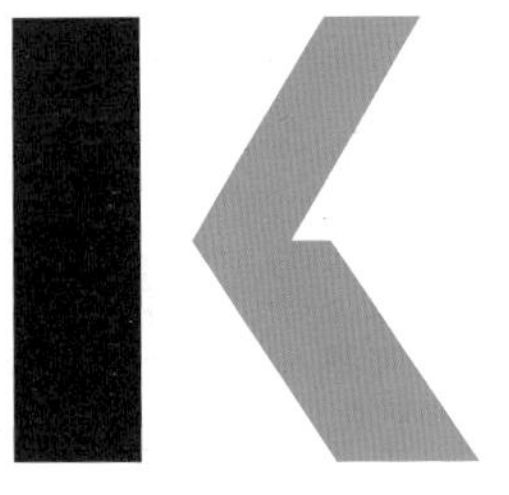

Kaplan Publishing are constantly finding new ways to make a difference to your studies and our exciting online resources really do offer something different to students looking for

This book comes with free MyKapla that you can study anytime, anywh

Having purchased this book, you have access to the following online study materials:

CONTENT	ACCA (including FFA,FAB,FMA)		AAT		FIA (excluding FFA,FAB,FMA)	
	Text	Kit	Text	Kit	Text	Kit
iPaper version of the book	✓	✓	✓	✓	✓	✓
Interactive electronic version of the book	✓					
Progress tests with instant answers	✓		✓			
Mock assessments online			✓	✓		
Material updates	✓	✓	✓	✓	✓	✓
Latest official ACCA exam questions		✓				
Extra question assistance using the signpost icon*		✓				
Timed questions with an online tutor debrief using the clock icon*		✓				
Interim assessment including questions and answers	✓				✓	
Technical articles	✓	✓			✓	✓

* Excludes F1, F2, F3, FFA, FAB, FMA

How to access your online resources

Kaplan Financial students will already have a MyKaplan account and these extra resources will be available to you online. You do not need to register again, as this process was completed when you enrolled. If you are having problems accessing online materials, please ask your course administrator.

If you are already a registered MyKaplan user go to www.MyKaplan.co.uk and log in. Select the 'add a book' feature and enter the ISBN number of this book and the unique pass key at the bottom of this card. Then click 'finished' or 'add another book'. You may add as many books as you have purchased from this screen.

If you purchased through Kaplan Flexible Learning or via the Kaplan Publishing website you will automatically receive an e-mail invitation to MyKaplan. Please register your details using this email to gain access to your content. If you do not receive the e-mail or book content, please contact Kaplan Flexible Learning.

If you are a new MyKaplan user register at www.MyKaplan.co.uk and click on the link contained in the email we sent you to activate your account. Then select the 'add a book' feature, enter the ISBN number of this book and the unique pass key at the bottom of this card. Then click 'finished' or 'add another book'.

Your Code and Information

This code can only be used once for the registration of one book online. This registration and your online content will expire when the final sittings for the examinations covered by this book have taken place. Please allow one hour from the time you submit your book details for us to process your request.

Please scratch the film to access your MyKaplan code.

Please be aware that this code is case-sensitive and you will need to include the dashes within the passcode, but not when entering the ISBN. For further technical support, please visit www.MyKaplan.co.uk

Professional Examinations

AQ2013 Level 3

Costs and Revenues

REVISION KIT

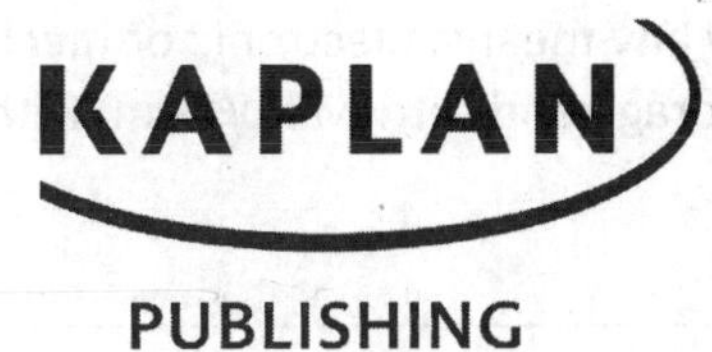

British Library Cataloguing-in-Publication Data

A catalogue record for this book is available from the British Library.

Published by:

Kaplan Publishing UK

Unit 2 The Business Centre

Molly Millar's Lane

Wokingham

Berkshire

RG41 2QZ

ISBN: 978-0-85732-895-3

Printed and bound in Great Britain

CONTENTS

Features in this revision kit

In addition to providing a wide ranging bank of real exam style questions, we have also included in this kit:

- Paper specific information and advice on exam technique.
- Our recommended approach to make your revision for this particular subject as effective as possible.

You will find a wealth of other resources to help you with your studies on the AAT website:

www.aat.org.uk/

INDEX TO QUESTIONS AND ANSWERS

EXAM TECHNIQUE

- **Do not skip any of the material** in the syllabus.
- **Read each question** *very* carefully.
- **Double-check your answer** before committing yourself to it.
- Answer **every** question – if you do not know an answer to a multiple choice question or true/false question, you don't lose anything by guessing. Think carefully before you **guess**.
- If you are answering a multiple-choice question, **eliminate first those answers that you know are wrong**. Then choose the most appropriate answer from those that are left.
- **Don't panic** if you realise you've answered a question incorrectly. Getting one question wrong will not mean the difference between passing and failing

Computer-based exams – tips

- Do not attempt a CBA until you have **completed all study material** relating to it.
- On the AAT website there is a CBA demonstration. It is **ESSENTIAL** that you attempt this before your real CBA. You will become familiar with how to move around the CBA screens and the way that questions are formatted, increasing your confidence and speed in the actual exam.
- Be sure you understand how to use the **software** before you start the exam. If in doubt, ask the assessment centre staff to explain it to you.
- Questions are **displayed on the screen** and answers are entered using keyboard and mouse. At the end of the exam, you are given a certificate showing the result you have achieved.
- In addition to the traditional multiple-choice question type, CBAs will also contain **other types of questions**, such as number entry questions, drag and drop, true/false, pick lists or drop down menus or hybrids of these.
- You need to be sure you **know how to answer questions** of this type before you sit the exam, through practice.

PAPER SPECIFIC INFORMATION

THE EXAM

FORMAT OF THE ASSESSMENT

The assessment will comprise ten independent tasks. Students will normally be assessed by computer-based assessment.

Task	Title for topics within task range
1	Inventory control
2	Cost accounting journal entries
3	Calculation of direct labour costs
4	Overhead allocation and apportionment
5	Overhead absorption/Choice of costing principles
6	Activity effects/segmental reporting
7	Break-even (CVP) analysis
8	Limiting factor decision making/Types of costing systems
9	Variance analysis
10	Capital investment appraisal

Time allowed

2 ½ hours

PASS MARK

The pass mark for all AAT CBAs is 70%.

 **Always keep your eye on the clock and make sure you attempt all questions!**

DETAILED SYLLABUS

The detailed syllabus and study guide written by the AAT can be found at:

www.aat.org.uk/

KAPLAN'S RECOMMENDED REVISION APPROACH

QUESTION PRACTICE IS THE KEY TO SUCCESS

Success in professional examinations relies upon you acquiring a firm grasp of the required knowledge at the tuition phase. In order to be able to do the questions, knowledge is essential.

However, the difference between success and failure often hinges on your exam technique on the day and making the most of the revision phase of your studies.

The **Kaplan textbook** is the starting point, designed to provide the underpinning knowledge to tackle all questions. However, in the revision phase, poring over text books is not the answer.

The Kaplan workbook helps you consolidate your knowledge and understanding and is a useful tool to check whether you can remember key topic areas.

Kaplan pocket notes are designed to help you quickly revise a topic area, however you then need to practise questions. There is a need to progress to exam style questions as soon as possible, and to tie your exam technique and technical knowledge together.

The importance of question practice cannot be over-emphasised.

The recommended approach below is designed by expert tutors in the field, in conjunction with their knowledge of the examiner and the specimen assessment.

You need to practise as many questions as possible in the time you have left.

OUR AIM

Our aim is to get you to the stage where you can attempt exam questions confidently, to time, in a closed book environment, with no supplementary help (i.e. to simulate the real examination experience).

Practising your exam technique is also vitally important for you to assess your progress and identify areas of weakness that may need more attention in the final run up to the examination.

In order to achieve this we recognise that initially you may feel the need to practice some questions with open book help.

Good exam technique is vital.

THE KAPLAN CSTR REVISION PLAN

Stage 1: Assess areas of strengths and weaknesses

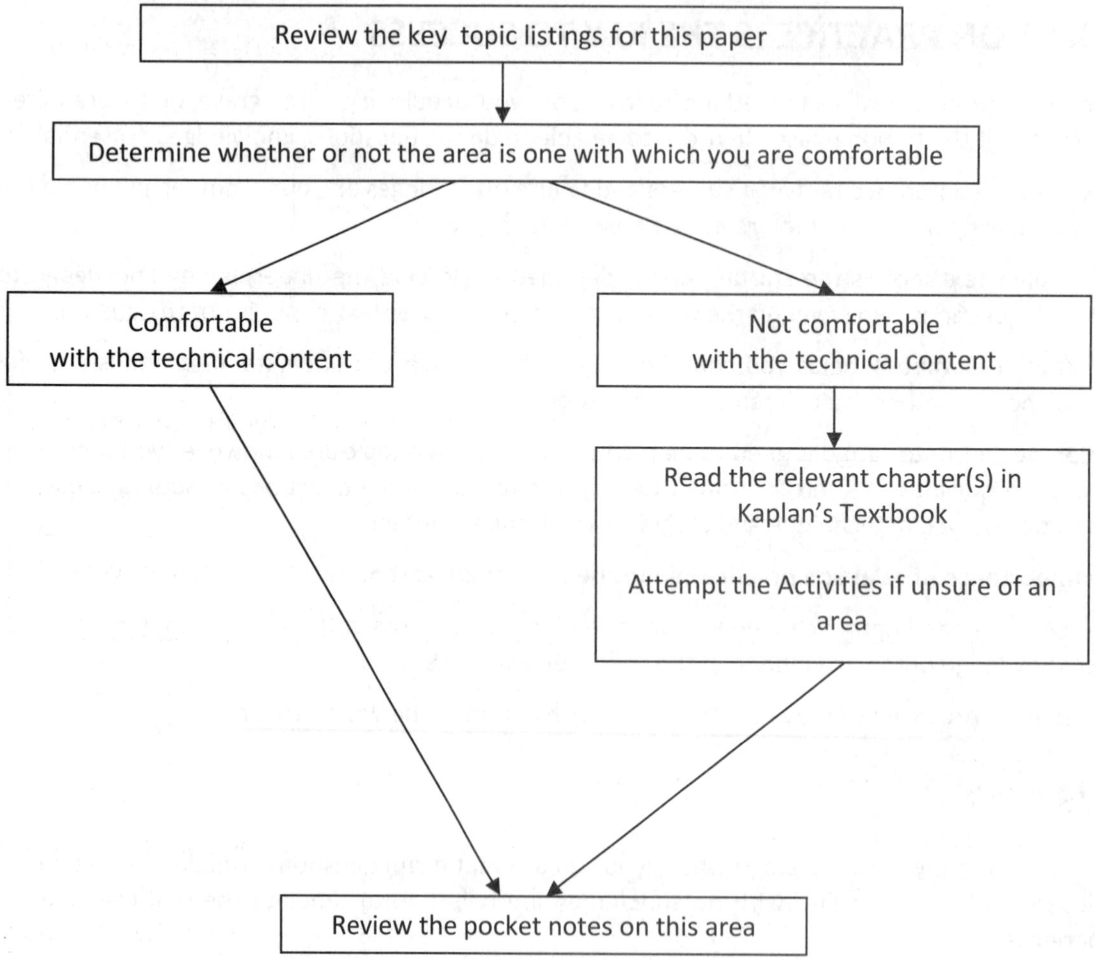

Stage 2: Practise questions

Follow the order of revision of topics as presented in this kit and attempt the questions in the order suggested.

Try to avoid referring to text books and notes and the model answer until you have completed your attempt.

Review your attempt with the model answer and assess how much of the answer you achieved.

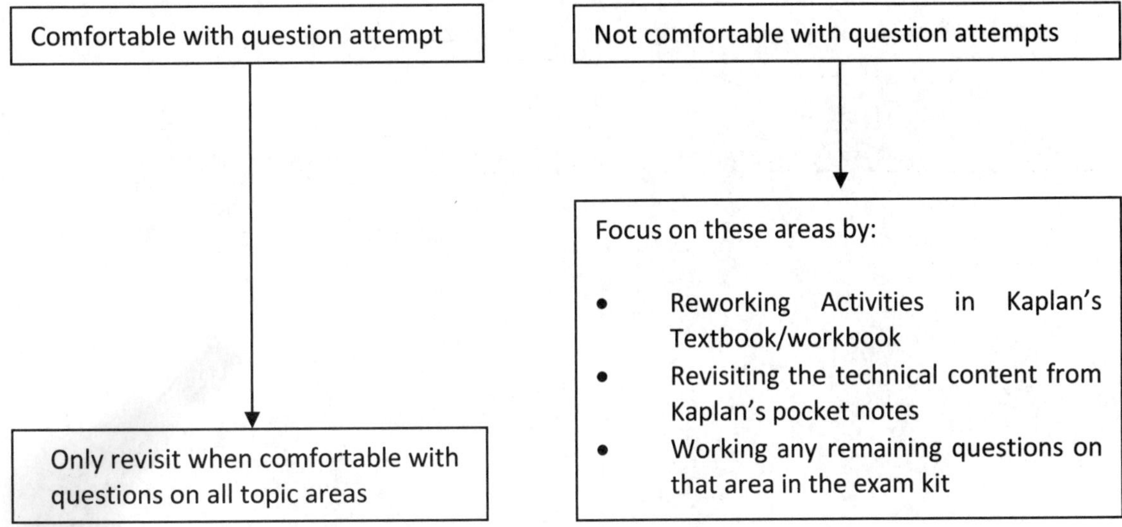

Stage 3: Final pre-exam revision

We recommend that you **attempt at least one two and a half hour mock examination** containing a set of previously unseen exam standard questions.

Attempt the mock CBA online in timed, closed book conditions to simulate the real exam experience

Stage 2: Practice questions

[illegible]

Section 1

PRACTICE QUESTIONS

INVENTORY

1 Which of the following is least relevant to the simple economic order quantity model for inventory?

A Safety inventory

B Annual demand

C Holding costs

D Ordering costs

2 The EOQ formula includes the cost of placing an order. However, the management accountant is unsure which of the following items would usually be included in 'cost of placing an order'

(i) administrative costs

(ii) postage

(iii) quality control costs

(iv) unit cost of products

(v) storekeeper's salary

Which three if the above would be regarded as part of the cost of placing an order?

A (i), (ii) and (iii)

B (i), (iv) and (v)

C (ii), (iii) and (iv)

D (i), (ii) and (v)

3 A business, which orders 500 units each time, has looked at the delivery time and usage for the raw material and it has the following data:

Usage: between 500 and 800 a week

Lead time: between 1 and 3 weeks

- Calculate the maximum inventory level:
- Calculate the minimum inventory level:

4 PLASTIC

The following information is available for plastic grade PM7:

- Annual demand 112,500 kilograms.
- Annual holding cost per kilogram £1.80
- Fixed ordering cost £3.60

(a) **Calculate the Economic Order Quantity (EOQ) for PM7 (round to the nearest whole number)**

The inventory record shown below for plastic grade PM7 for the month of July has only been fully completed for the first three weeks of the month.

(b) **Complete the entries in the inventory record for the two receipts on 24 and 28 July that were ordered using the EOQ method.**

(c) **Complete ALL entries in the inventory record for the two issues in the month and for the closing balance at the end of July using the FIFO method of issuing inventory.**

(Show the costs per kilogram (kg) in £'s to 3 decimal places; and the total costs in whole £'s).

Inventory record for plastic grade PM7

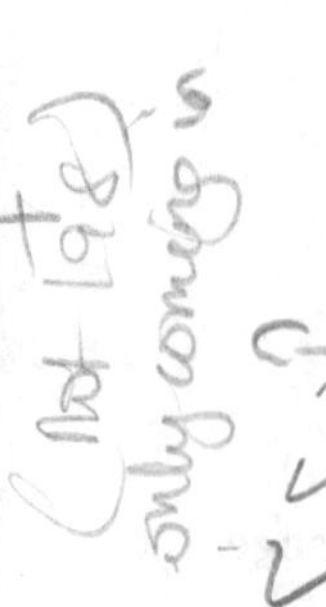

	Receipts			*Issues*			*Balance*	
Date	*Quantity kgs*	*Cost per kg (£)*	*Total cost (£)*	*Quantity kgs*	*Cost per kg (£)*	*Total cost (£)*	*Quantity kgs*	*Total cost (£)*
Balance as at 22 July							198	238
24 July		2.336						
26 July				540				
28 July		2.344						
30 July				710				

(d) **Using the LIFO method, the issue of 540 kg to production on the 26 July would be valued at a total of ____________________.**

5 SURESTICK GLUE

The following information is available for direct material SURESTICK GLUE:

- Fixed ordering cost £2.50
- Annual holding cost per litre £1.00
- Monthly demand 2,500 litres

(a) **Calculate the Economic Order Quantity (EOQ) for direct material SURESTICK GLUE (round your answer up to the nearest whole number)**

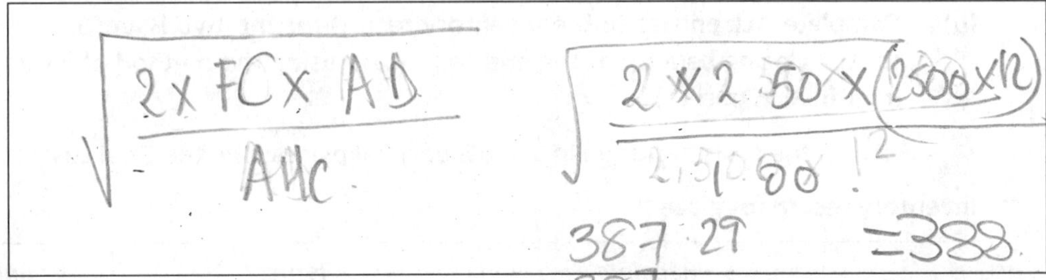

The inventory record shown below for SURESTICK GLUE for the month of June has only been fully completed for the first three weeks of the month.

(b) **Complete the entries in the inventory record for the two receipts on 24 and 27 June that were ordered using the EOQ method.**

(c) **Complete ALL entries in the inventory record for the two issues in the month and for the closing balance at the end of June using the AVCO method of issuing inventory.**

(Show the costs per litre in £'s to 3 decimal places; and the total costs in whole £'s, round up to nearest whole number).

Inventory record for SURESTICK GLUE

	Receipts			*Issues*			*Balance*	
Date	*Quantity litres*	*Cost per litre (£)*	*Total cost (£)*	*Quantity litres*	*Cost per litre (£)*	*Total cost (£)*	*Quantity Litres*	*Total cost (£)*
Balance as at 23 June							65	130
24 June		2.234						
26 June				180				
27 June		2.341						
30 June				250				

(d) **Using the LIFO method, the issue of 180 kg to production on the 26 June would be valued at a total of ____________________.**

6 GRAPE LTD

The inventory record shown below for glaze for the month of January has only been fully completed for the first three weeks of the month.

(a) Identify the inventory valuation method used to complete the inventory record:

A FIFO

B LIFO

C AVCO

(b) Complete ALL entries in the inventory record for the two issues in the month and for the closing balance at the end of January using the method of issuing inventory identified in part (a)

(Show the costs per drum in £'s to 3 decimal places; and the total costs in whole £'s).

Inventory record for glaze

	Receipts			*Issues*			*Balance*	
Date	*Quantity drums*	*Cost per drum (£)*	*Total cost (£)*	*Quantity drums*	*Cost per drum (£)*	*Total cost (£)*	*Quantity drums*	*Total cost (£)*
Balance as at 22 January							1,650	1,980
25 January	1,200	1.250					2,850	3,480
26 January				1,300		1,587		
28 January	1,200	1.302						
31 January				1,500				

7 GLOBE LTD

(a) Identify the inventory valuation method used to complete the inventory record:

A FIFO

B LIFO

C AVCO

(b) **Complete ALL entries in the inventory record for the two issues in the month and for the closing balance at the end of March using the method of issuing inventory identified in part (a)**

(Show the costs per tonne in £'s to 2 decimal places; and the total costs in whole £'s).

Inventory record for M2

	Receipts			*Issues*			*Balance*	
Date	*Quantity tonnes*	*Cost per tonne (£)*	*Total cost (£)*	*Quantity tonnes*	*Cost per tonne (£)*	*Total cost (£)*	*Quantity tonnes*	*Total cost (£)*
Balance as at 27 March							1,200	14,400
28 March	800	12.50					2,000	24,400
29 March				820		9,840		
30 March	800	12.25						
31 March				900				

8 In a period of rising prices, which type of inventory valuation shows the highest profit?

A FIFO

B LIFO

C AVCO

D None

9 In times of rising prices, the valuation of inventory using the First In First Out method, as opposed to the Weighted Average Cost method, will result in which ONE of the following combinations?

	Cost of sales	*Profit*	*Closing inventory*
A	Lower	Higher	Higher
B	Lower	Higher	Lower
C	Higher	Lower	Higher
D	Higher	Higher	Lower

JOURNAL ENTRIES

INVENTORY

10 The following represent the materials transactions for a company for the month of December 20X6:

	£000s
Materials purchases	176
Issued to production	165
Materials written off	4
Returned to stores	9
Returned to suppliers	8

The material inventory at 1 December 20X6 was £15,000.

What is the closing balance on the materials inventory account at 31 December 20X6?

A £5,000

B £16,000

C £23,000

D £31,000

11 Put the correct entries into the Journal below to record the following FOUR accounting transactions:

1 Receipt of SURESTICK GLUE into inventory paying immediately by BACS.

2 Issue of SURESTICK GLUE from inventory to production.

3 Receipt of SURESTICK GLUE into inventory paying on credit.

4 Return of SURESTICK GLUE from production to inventory.

The choices are:

A Dr. Bank, Cr. Inventory

B Dr. Trade Payables' Control, Cr. Inventory

C Dr. Inventory, Cr. Bank

D Dr. Inventory, Cr. Trade Payables' Control

E Dr. Inventory, Cr. Production

F Dr. Production, Cr. Inventory

	Choice
Transaction 1	
Transaction 2	
Transaction 3	
Transaction 4	

12 Put the correct entries into the Journal below to record the following FOUR accounting transactions:

1 Receipt of glaze into inventory paying on credit.

2 Write off of glaze.

3 Receipt of glaze into inventory paying immediately by BACS.

4 Return of glaze to the supplier.

The choices are:

A Dr. Bank, Cr. Inventory

B Dr. Trade Payables' Control, Cr. Inventory

C Dr. Inventory, Cr. Bank

D Dr. Inventory, Cr. Trade Payables' Control

E Dr. Inventory, Cr. Production

F Dr. Statement of profit or loss, Cr. Inventory

	Choice
Transaction 1	
Transaction 2	
Transaction 3	
Transaction 4	

13 The double entry for an issue of indirect production materials would be:

A	Dr	Materials control account	Cr	Finished goods control account
B	Dr	Production overhead control a/c	Cr	Materials control account
C	Dr	Work-in-progress control account	Cr	Production overhead control a/c
D	Dr	Work-in-progress control account	Cr	Materials control account

LABOUR

14 The payroll for maintenance employees for the week ending 30 November has been completed. The following payments are to be made:

	£
Net wages/salaries to pay to employees	10,000
Income tax and national insurance contributions (NIC) to pay to HMRC	2,000
Pension contributions to pay to F4L pension scheme	1,000
Gross payroll costs	13,000

The payroll for the week is analysed as:

	£
Direct labour costs	7,000
Indirect labour costs	4,000
Maintenance administration labour costs	2,000
Gross payroll costs	13,000

The following cost account codes are used to record maintenance labour costs:

Code	*Description*
6200	Maintenance direct labour
6400	Maintenance overheads
6600	Maintenance administration
8200	Wages control

(a) **Complete the wages control account entries in the account shown below:**

Wages control account			
	£		£
Bank (net wages/salaries)		Maintenance (direct labour)	
HMRC (income tax and NIC)		Maintenance overheads	
Pension contributions		Maintenance administration	
	13,000		13,000

(b) **Complete the table below to show how the gross payroll cost for the week is charged to the various cost accounts of the business:**

Date	*Code*	*Debit*	*Credit*
30 November			
30 November			
30 November			
30 November			
30 November			
30 November			

15 Put the correct entries into the Journal below to record the following FOUR accounting transactions:

1 Record labour costs in the cost ledger

2 Analyse direct labour costs

3 Record indirect labour costs

4 Record additional production overheads

The choices are:

A Dr Wages control, Cr. Bank

B Dr Work-in-progress, Cr. Wages control

C Dr Production overhead account, Cr. Wages Control

D Dr Production overhead control, Cr. Bank

E Dr Inventory, Cr. Production

F Dr Production, Cr. Inventory

	Choice
Transaction 1	
Transaction 2	
Transaction 3	
Transaction 4	

OVERHEADS

16 At the end of a period, in an integrated cost and financial accounting system, the accounting entries for £10,000 overheads over-absorbed would be:

A	Dr	Work-in-progress control account	Cr	Overhead control account
B	Dr	Statement of profit or loss	Cr	Work-in-progress control account
C	Dr	Statement of profit or loss	Cr	Overhead control account
D	Dr	Overhead control account	Cr	Statement of profit or loss

17 During a period £50,000 was incurred for indirect labour. In a typical cost ledger, the double entry for this is:

A	Dr	Wages control	Cr	Overhead control
B	Dr	WIP control	Cr	Wages control
C	Dr	Overhead control	Cr	Wages control
D	Dr	Wages control	Cr	WIP control

LABOUR COSTS

LABOUR

18 CARTCYLE LTD

Below is a weekly timesheet for one of Cartcyle Ltd's employees, who is paid as follows:

- For a basic six-hour shift every day from Monday to Friday – basic pay.
- For any overtime in excess of the basic six hours, on any day from Monday to Friday – the extra hours are paid at time-and-a-half (basic pay plus an overtime premium equal to half of basic pay).
- For three contracted hours each Saturday morning – basic pay.
- For any hours in excess of three hours on Saturday – the extra hours are paid at double time (basic pay plus an overtime premium equal to basic pay).
- For any hours worked on Sunday – paid at double time (basic pay plus an overtime premium equal to basic pay).

Complete the columns headed Basic pay, Overtime premium and Total pay:

(***Notes:*** Zero figures should be entered in cells where appropriate)

Employee's weekly timesheet for week ending 7 December

Employee:	A.Man		**Profit Centre:**	Wood finishing		
Employee number:	C812		**Basic pay per hour:**	£8.00		
	Hours spent on production	*Hours worked on indirect work*	*Notes*	*Basic pay* £	*Overtime premium* £	*Total pay* £
Monday	6	2	10am–12am cleaning of machinery			
Tuesday	2	4	9am–1pm customer care course			
Wednesday	8					
Thursday	6					
Friday	6	1	3–4pm health and safety training			
Saturday	6					
Sunday	3					
Total	**37**	**7**				

19 A company employs a group of production workers who, as well as earning basic pay, are also paid a weekly group bonus based on their productivity during each week.

The group has a standard (target) output of 800 units of production per hour worked. All output in excess of this level earns a bonus for each of the employees.

The bonus % is calculated as:

$$25\% \times \frac{\text{Excess production (units)}}{\text{Standard production (units)}} \times 100$$

The bonus rate per hour is then calculated as: bonus % × £10.

The following information relates to this group's performance last week:

	Hours worked	*Actual production (units)*
Monday	920	940,000
Tuesday	870	890,000
Wednesday	910	930,000
Thursday	920	960,000
Friday	940	990,000
Saturday	440	690,000
Total	5,000	5,400,000

(a) **Use the table below to calculate the group bonus rate per hour and the total bonus to be paid to the group.**

	Units
Actual production	
Less standard production (based on actual hours worked)	
Excess production	
Bonus %	
Group bonus rate per hour £	
Total group bonus £	

(b) **An employee in this group worked for 44 hours last week, and is paid a basic rate of £9.60 per hour. The employee's total pay for last week was:**

£

20 GRAPES

Below is a weekly timesheet for one of Grape's employees, who is paid as follows:

- For a basic seven-hour shift every day from Monday to Friday – basic pay.
- For any overtime in excess of the basic seven hours, on any day from Monday to Friday – the extra hours are paid at basic pay plus an overtime premium is added of 50% of basic pay.
- For two contracted hours each Saturday morning – basic pay.
- For any hours in excess of two hours on Saturday – the overtime premium is paid at 75% of basic pay.

Complete the columns headed Basic pay, Overtime premium and Total pay:

(***Notes:*** Zero figures should be entered in cells where appropriate)

Employee's weekly timesheet for week ending 31 January

Employee:	Olivia Michael		**Profit Centre:**		Moulding Department	
Employee number:	P450		**Basic pay per hour:**		£10.00	
	Hours spent in work	*Hours spent on indirect work*	*Notes*	*Basic pay* £	*Overtime premium* £	*Total pay* £
Monday	8	3	10am–1pm cleaning moulds			
Tuesday	7	4	9am–1pm fire training			
Wednesday	8					
Thursday	7	1				
Friday	7	1	3–4pm annual appraisal			
Saturday	3					
Total	**40**	**9**				

Analysis the timesheet into production and production overhead costs

Labour cost account

	£		£
Bank		Production	
		Production Overheads	

21 **The following information relates to direct labour costs incurred in producing 57,600 labelled soft drink bottles during May:**

Normal time hours worked	900 hours
Overtime at time and a half worked	180 hours
Overtime at double time worked	135 hours
Total hours worked	1,215 hours
Normal time hourly rate	£8 per hour

Overtime premiums paid are included as part of direct labour cost.

A trainee accounts clerk has produced the following incorrect calculation of the total cost of direct labour used to produce these bottles:

	£
Cost at normal rate – 1,215 hours at £8 =	9,720
Cost at time and a half – 135 hours at £12 =	1,620
Cost at double time – 180 hours at £16 =	2,880
Total direct labour cost	**14,220**

(a) **Calculate the correct total cost of direct labour used to produce the bottles during May.**

£

(b) **Calculate the direct labour cost per soft drink bottle.**

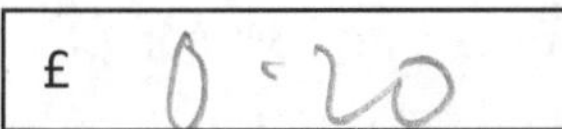

22 **A company operates a piecework system of remuneration. Employees must work for a minimum of 37 hours per week. Sebastian produces the following output for a particular week:**

Product	*Quantity*	*Standard time per item (hours)*	*Total actual time (hours)*
Buckles	50	0.2	9
Press studs	200	0.06	14
Belts	100	0.1	12
Buttons	10	0.7	6
			41

Sebastian is paid £8.00 per standard hour worked. What are his earnings for the week?

A £296

B £302

C £312

D £328

23 (a) **information is available relating to the production of the tins of cat food for the month of july:**

Total number of labour hours worked	10,800
Overtime hours worked	2,450
Standard hours for production in October	11,200
Normal rate per hour	£9
Overtime payment per hour	£14.50

The company operates a group incentive scheme, whereby a bonus of 35% of the normal hourly rate is paid for hours saved.

Calculate the total cost of direct labour for July, assuming that overtime and the bonus are due to a specific customer request.

Total basic pay (£)	
Total overtime premium (£)	
Hours saved (hours)	
Bonus (£)	
Total direct labour cost (£)	

(b) **In August the bonus was based on equivalent units. Employees will receive 45% of the basic hourly rate for every equivalent unit in excess of target. Rates of pay are not due to change in August. The target production is 450 units.**

At the end of August 300 units were completed and there were 200 units of closing work in progress that was 100% complete for material and 75% complete for labour.

Calculate the number of equivalent units with regards to labour and the bonus payable

Equivalent units	
Bonus (£)	

ACCOUNTING FOR OVERHEADS

OVERHEAD ALLOCATION AND APPORTIONMENT

24 What is cost apportionment?

A The charging of discrete identifiable items of cost to cost centres or cost units

B The collection of costs attributable to cost centres and cost units using the costing methods, principles and techniques prescribed for a particular business entity

C The process of establishing the costs of cost centres or cost units

D The division of costs amongst two or more cost centres in proportion to the estimated benefit received, using a proxy, e.g. square feet

25 CARTCYLE LTD

Cartcyle Ltd's budgeted overheads for the next financial year are:

	£	£
Depreciation of plant and equipment		1,447,470
Power for production machinery		1,287,000
Rent and rates		188,100
Light and heat		41,580
Indirect labour costs:		
Maintenance	182,070	
Stores	64,890	
Administration	432,180	
Total indirect labour cost		679,140

The following information is also available:

Department	*Carrying value of plant and equipment.*	*Production machinery power usage (KwH)*	*Floor space (square metres)*	*Number of employees*
Production:				
Wood cutting	10,080,000	3,861,000		25
Wood finishing	4,320,000	2,574,000		18
Support:				
Maintenance			25,200	9
Stores			15,120	3
Administration			10,080	12
Total	14,400,000	6,435,000	50,400	67

Overheads are allocated or apportioned on the most appropriate basis. The total overheads of the support cost centres are then reapportioned to the two production centres using the direct method.

- 70% of the Maintenance cost centre's time is spent maintaining production machinery in the Wood cutting production centre and the remainder in the Wood finishing production centre.
- The Stores cost centre makes 65% of its issues to the Wood cutting production centre, and 35% to the Wood finishing production centre.
- Administration supports the two production centres equally.

There is no reciprocal servicing between the three support cost centres.

Complete the overhead analysis table below:

	Basis of apportionment	Wood cutting	Wood Finishing	Maintenance	Stores	Admin	Totals
		£	£	£	£	£	£
Depreciation of plant and equipment							
Power for production machinery							
Rent and rates							
Light and heat							
Indirect labour							
Totals							
Reapportion Maintenance							
Reapportion Stores							
Reapportion Admin.							
Total overheads to production centres							

26 AQUARIOUS

Aquarious Ltd's budgeted overheads for the next financial year are:

	£	£
Depreciation of plant and equipment		700,000
Power for production machinery		620,000
Rent and rates		100,000
Light and heat		20,000
Indirect labour costs:		
Maintenance	102,000	
Stores	40,000	
Administration	240,000	
Total indirect labour cost		382,000

The following information is also available:

Department	*Carrying value of plant and equipment.*	*Production machinery power usage (KwH)*	*Floor space (square metres)*	*Number of employees*
Production:				
Assembly	4,440,000	2,210,000		10
Finishing	2,960,000	1,190,000		10
Support:				
Maintenance			12,000	6
Stores			8,000	4
Administration			5,000	8
Total	7,400,000	3,400,000	25,000	38

Overheads are allocated or apportioned on the most appropriate basis. The total overheads of the support cost centres are then reapportioned to the two production centres using the direct method.

- The overhead allocated and apportioned to Administration is re-apportioned to the other production and support cost centres based on the number of employees.
- The Stores cost centre makes 50% of its issues to the Assembly production centre, 30% to the Finishing production centre and 20% to Maintenance.
- 75% of the Maintenance cost centre's time is spent maintaining production machinery in the Assembly production centre and the remainder in the Finishing production centre.

Complete the overhead analysis table below:

	Basis of apportionment	Assembly	Finishing	Maintenance	Stores	Admin	Totals
		£	£	£	£	£	£
Depreciation of plant and equipment	CV	42,000					700,000
Power for production machinery	PMP						620,000
Rent and rates	FS						100,000
Light and heat	FS						20,000
Indirect labour	Allocate			102,000	40,000	240,000	382,000
Totals							
Reapportion Admin.							
Reapportion Stores							
Reapportion Maintenance							
Total overheads to production centres							

27 F4L has budgeted for the following overheads for its two profit and three cost centres for quarter 1 of the next financial year:

	£000	£000
Depreciation of aircraft		36,400
Aviation fuel and other variable costs		42,200
Pilots and aircrew salaries:		
Scheduled services	5,250	
Charter flights	4,709	
Total pilots and aircrew salaries		9,959
Rent and rates and other premises costs		12,600
Indirect labour costs:		
Aircraft maintenance and repairs	9,600	
Fuel and parts store	3,200	
General administration	7,800	
Total indirect labour cost		20,600

The following information is also available:

Profit/cost centre	*Carrying amount of aircraft (£000)*	*Planned number of miles flown*	*Floor space (square metres)*	*Number of employees*
Scheduled services	1,080,000	215,600		105
Charter flights	720,000	176,400		96
Aircraft maintenance and repairs			190,000	260
Fuel and parts store			114,000	146
General administration			76,000	220
Total	1,800,000	392,000	380,000	827

Primary allocations or apportionments are made on the most appropriate basis. The support cost centres are then reapportioned to the two flight profit centres using the direct method.

- The Aircraft maintenance and repairs cost centre spends 60% of its time maintaining the aircraft in the scheduled services profit centre and the remainder in the charter flights profit centre.
- 55% of the issues from the Fuel and parts store cost centre is made to the scheduled services profit centre and the remainder to the charter flights profit centre.
- The scheduled services profit centre and the charter flights profit centre both incur general administration costs equally.
- The three support cost centres are not involved in reciprocal servicing.

Use the following table to allocate or apportion the overheads between the profit/cost centres, using the most appropriate basis.

	Basis of apportionment	Scheduled services	Charter flights	Aircraft maintenance and repairs	Fuel and parts store	General admin.	Totals
		£000	£000	£000	£000	£000	£000
Depreciation of aircraft							
Aviation fuel and other variable costs							
Pilots and aircrew salaries							
Rent and rates and other premises costs							
Indirect labour							
Totals							
Reapportion Aircraft maintenance and repairs							
Reapportion Fuel and parts store							
Reapportion General admin.							
Total overheads to profit centres							

28 Premier Labels Ltd produces labelled plastic food containers. The budgeted overheads for the next quarter are shown below, together with their behaviour and how they are apportioned to departments.

Budgeted cost	*Cost behaviour*	£	*Comments*
Heat and lighting	Semi-variable	60,000	Apportion fixed element of £24,000 equally between all four departments. Apportion variable element according to floor area.
Power for machinery	Variable	28,000	Apportion 70% to Plastics Moulding, and 30% to Labelling.
Supervision	Fixed	120,000	Apportion to the two production departments pro rata to direct labour costs.
Stores wages	Fixed	72,000	
Equipment Maintenance salaries	Fixed	188,200	
Depreciation of non-current assets	Fixed	84,000	Apportion according to carrying value of non-current assets.
Other overhead costs	Dependant on specific cost	128,000	Apportion 60% to Plastics Moulding, 20% to Labelling, and 10% each to Stores and Equipment Maintenance.

The following information is also available:

Department	*Square metres occupied*	*Carrying value of non-current assets* (£)	*Number of material requisitions*	*Direct labour costs* (£)
Plastics Moulding	320,000	160,000	162,750	100,000
Labelling	180,000	80,000	56,000	140,000
Stores	80,000	30,000		
Equipment Maintenance	20,000	10,000		

Notes: The Equipment Maintenance department's total costs should be apportioned equally to the other three departments. Then the total of the Stores department's costs should be apportioned according to the number of material requisitions.

Complete the overhead analysis table below:

	Basis of apportionment	Plastics Moulding	Labelling	Stores	Equipment Maintenance	Totals
Heat and lighting fixed cost						
Heat and lighting variable cost						
Power for machinery						
Supervision						
Stores wages						
Equipment maintenance salaries						
Depreciation of non-current assets						
Other overhead costs						
Totals						
Reapportion Equipment maintenance						
Reapportion stores						
Total overheads to profit centres						

OVERHEAD ABSORPTION

29 An overhead absorption rate is used to:

A share out common costs over benefiting cost centres

B find the total overheads for a cost centre

C charge overheads to products

D control overheads

30 Cartcycle Ltd's budgeted overheads in the wood cutting department were £586,792. The overheads are absorbed based on machine hours. The budgeted machine hours were 9,464 and the actual machine hours were 9,745. The actual overhead cost was £568,631

(a) **What is the overhead absorption rate?**

A £62 per machine hour

B £60 per machine hour

C £58 per machine hour

D £55 per machine hour

(b) **How much overhead was absorbed?**

A £584,700

B £586,768

C £604,190

D £565,210

(c) **What is the under or over absorbed amount?**

A £35,559 over

B £35,599 under

C £21,582 over

D £21,582 under

31 Next quarter Aquarious Ltd's budgeted overheads and activity levels are:

	Assembly	*Finishing*
Budgeted overheads (£)	155,000	105,000
Budgeted direct labour hours	12,500	8,750
Budgeted machine hours	2,000	1,750

(a) **What would the budgeted overhead absorption rate be for each department, if this were set based on their both being heavily automated?**

A Assembly £77.50/hour, Finishing £12/hour

B Assembly £77.50/hour, Finishing £60/hour

C Assembly £12.40/hour, Finishing £60/hour

D Assembly £12.40/hour, Finishing £12/hour

(b) **What would the budgeted overhead absorption rate be for each department, if this were set based on their both being labour intensive?**

A Assembly £77.50/hour, Finishing £12/hour

B Assembly £77.50/hour, Finishing £60/hour

C Assembly £12.40/hour, Finishing £60/hour

D Assembly £12.40/hour, Finishing £12/hour

Additional data

At the end of the quarter actual overheads incurred in the finishing department were £119,000. Overheads were recovered on a machine hour basis. The machine hours worked were 10% less than budgeted.

(c) **What was the under or over absorptions for finishing in the quarter?**

£ ______________ under/over absorbed

32 Next quarter Grape Limited's budgeted overheads and activity levels are:

	Moulding Dept	*Painting Dept*
Budgeted overheads (£)	36,000	39,000
Budgeted direct labour hours	9,000	13,000
Budgeted machine hours	18,000	1,200

(a) **What would the budgeted overhead absorption rate be for each department, if the most appropriate basis was chosen?**

A Moulding £2/hour, Painting £32.50/hour

B Moulding £32.50/hour, Painting £2/hour

C Moulding £3/hour, Painting £33/hour

D Moulding £2/hour, Painting £3/hour

Additional data

At the end of the quarter actual overheads incurred were found to be:

	Moulding Dept	*Painting Dept*
Actual overheads (£)	37,500	40,000
Actual direct labour hours	9,500	13,500
Actual machine hours	17,500	700

(b) **How much overhead has been absorbed by each department?**

A Moulding £35,000, Painting £40,500

B Moulding £37,500 Painting £40,000

C Moulding £19,000, Painting £2,100

D Moulding £36,000, Painting £39,000

(c) **Using your answer from b what are the under or over absorptions in the quarter?**

A Moulding over absorbed £2,500, Painting over absorbed £500

B Moulding under absorbed £2,500, Painting over absorbed £500

C Moulding over absorbed £2,500, Painting under absorbed £500

D Moulding under absorbed £2,500, Painting under absorbed £500

33 **Next quarter Globe Limited's budgeted overheads and activity levels are:**

	Mixing Dept	*Bagging Dept*
Budgeted overheads (£)	64,800	70,200
Budgeted direct labour hours	1,620	2,340
Actual direct labour hours	1,840	2,120
Budgeted machine hours	10,000	12,000
Actual machine hours	9,000	13,000

(a) **What would the budgeted overhead absorption rate for each department, if the mixing department was heavily automated and the bagging department was labour intensive?**

A Mixing £6.48/hour, Bagging £30.00/hour

B Mixing £7.20/hour, Bagging £33.11/hour

C Mixing £6.48/hour, Bagging £5.85/hour

D Mixing £5.00/hour, Bagging £5.00/hour

(b) **How much overhead has been absorbed by production in each department?**

A Mixing £13,248, Bagging £70,193

B Mixing £58,320, Bagging £76,050

C Mixing £58,320, Bagging £63,600

D Mixing £64,800, Bagging £70,200

Additional data

At the end of the quarter actual overheads incurred were found to be:

	Mixing Dept	*Bagging Dept*
Actual overheads (£)	67,500	75,600

(c) **Using your answer from b what are the under or over absorptions in the quarter?**

A Mixing under absorbed £9,180, Bagging over absorbed £12,000

B Mixing under absorbed £9,180, Bagging under absorbed £12,000

C Mixing over absorbed £9,180, Bagging over absorbed £12,000

D Mixing over absorbed £9,180, Bagging under absorbed £12,000

34 Over-absorbed overheads occur when:

A absorbed overheads exceed actual overheads

B absorbed overheads exceed budgeted overheads

C actual overheads exceed budgeted overheads

D budgeted overheads exceed absorbed overheads

35 The management accountant's report shows that fixed production overheads were over-absorbed in the last accounting period. The combination that is certain to lead to this situation is:

A production volume is lower than budget and actual expenditure is higher than budget

B production volume is higher than budget and actual expenditure is higher than budget

C production volume and actual cost are as budgeted

D production volume is higher than budget and actual expenditure is lower than budget

ACTIVITY EFFECTS

COST BEHAVIOURS

36 The following data relate to two output levels of a department:

Machine hours	17,000	18,500
Overheads	£246,500	£251,750

The amount of fixed overheads is:

A £5,250

B £59,500

C £187,000

D £246,500

37 A manufacturing company has four types of cost (identified as T1, T2, T3 and T4).

The total cost for each type at two different production levels is:

Cost type	*Total cost for 125 units*	*Total cost for 180 units*
T1	£	£
T1	1,000	1,260
T2	1,750	2,520
T3	2,475	2,826
T4	3,225	4,644

Which two cost types would be classified as being semi-variable?

A T1 and T3

B T1 and T4

C T2 and T3

D T2 and T4

38 **Identify the TWO types of cost behaviour shown below:**

Total cost £

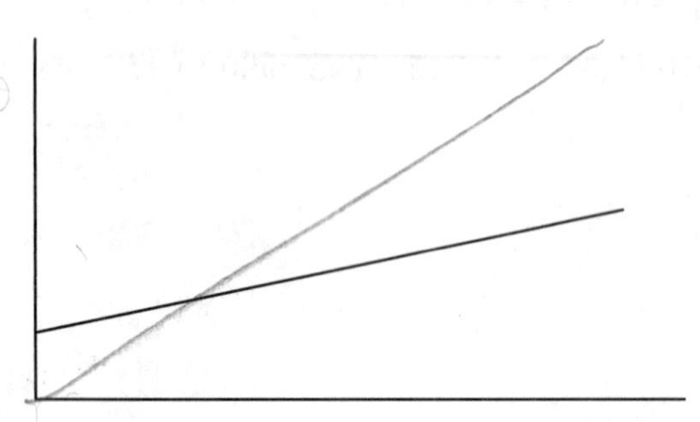

Activity

A Variable

B Fixed

C Semi variable

D Stepped fixed

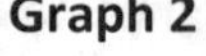

Total cost £

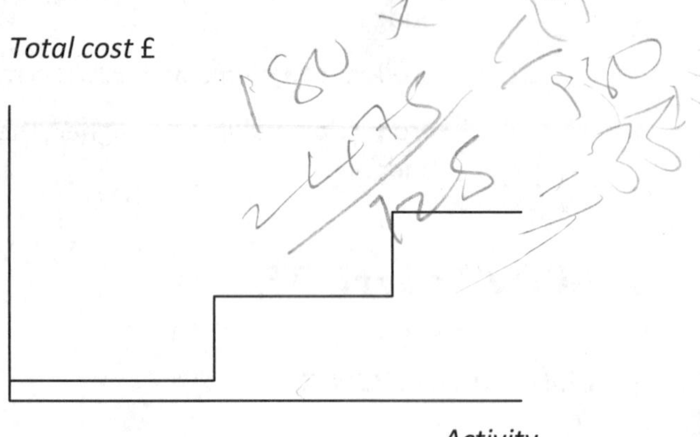

Activity

A Variable

B Fixed

C Semi variable

D Stepped fixed

39 Fill in the blanks using the words listed below:

________ costs are ones that can be economically and exclusively identified with a cost unit. Examples include __________ used in production of clothing and ________ used in the manufacture of computers.

________ costs, or _______, are costs that cannot be economically and exclusively identified with a cost unit. Examples include _________.

Direct   Indirect   Fabric   Overheads

Light, heat and power costs   Electrical components

40 Cartcyle Ltd has prepared a forecast for the next quarter for one of its wooden products, DR43. This component is produced in batches and the forecast is based on selling and producing 2,160 batches.

One of the customers of Cartcyle Ltd has indicated that it may be significantly increasing its order level for product DR43 for the next quarter and it appears that activity levels of 2,700 batches and 3,600 batches are feasible.

The semi-variable costs should be calculated using the high-low method. If 5,400 batches are sold the total semi-variable cost will be £13,284, and there is a constant unit variable cost up to this volume.

Complete the table below and calculate the estimated profit per batch of DR43 at the different activity levels.

Batches produced and sold	2,160	2,700	3,600
	£	£	£
Sales revenue	64,800		
Variable costs:			
• Direct materials	9,720		
• Direct labour	22,680		
• Overheads	12,960		
Semi-variable costs:	6,804		
• Variable element			
• Fixed element			
Total cost	52,164		
Total profit	12,636		
Profit per batch (to 2 decimal places)	5.85		

41 Charter Flights profit centre has just revised its forecasts for the number of miles it expects to fly during the next month on a particular charter contract. Originally it expected the contract would be for flights totalling 5,000 miles. Charter Flights now expects that the total miles to be flown will increase to either 6,000 or 7,000 miles.

Notes:

- The company chartering the flights has negotiated with Charter Flights a reduction of 10% per mile, paid on all miles flown in excess of the 5,000 miles agreed in the original contract.
- Landing and servicing fees are a semi-variable cost. There is a fixed charge of £600,000 plus £50/mile.

Complete the table below and calculate the estimated profit per batch of DR43 at the different activity levels.

Likely miles	5,000	6,000	7,000
	£000	£000	£000
Sale revenue	2,500		
Variable/semi-variable costs:			
• Aviation fuel	400		
• Landing and servicing fees	850		
• Other variable overheads	135		
Fixed costs:			
• Wages and salaries	420		
• Other fixed overheads	625		
Total cost	2430		
Total profit	70		
Profit per mile flown (2 decimal places) £	14.00		

42 Grape Ltd is negotiating a new contract with a customer for one of its products – The Owl. Owl is produced in batches and the forecast is based on selling and producing 800 batches.

The customer has indicated that it may be increasing its order level for Owl for the next quarter and it appears that activity levels of 1,200 units and 1,500 units are feasible.

The semi-variable costs should be calculated using the high-low method. If 1,600 batches are sold the total semi-variable cost will be £4,920, and there is a constant unit variable cost up to this volume.

Revenues and costs for 800 Owls are shown below. Fixed costs remain constant through the range being considered.

Units produced and sold	800
	£
Sales revenue	24,000
Variable costs:	
• Direct materials	3,600
• Direct labour	8,400
• Overheads	1,800
Semi-variable costs	2,520
Total cost	16,320
Total profit	7,680
Profit per batch (to 2 decimal places)	9.60

Calculate the following:

(a) The sales revenue per unit if the contract is for 800 Owls

(b) The variable cost per unit if the contract is for 1,200 Owls

(c) The fixed cost per unit if the contract is for 1,200 Owls

(d) The total cost per unit if the contract is for 1,500 Owls

(e) The profit per unit if the contract is for 1,500 Owls

SEGMENTAL REPORTS

43 India Ltd manufactures and sells three ranges of pottery, Rose, Tulip and Buttercup. The following information has been provided for the next quarter.

	Rose	*Tulip*	*Buttercup*
Sales revenue (£)	50,000	24,000	40,000
Direct materials (£)	10,000	4,800	8,000
Direct labour (£)	13,000	8,800	10,500

India Ltd expects to produce and sell 1,000 units of Rose and 200 units of Tulip. The budgeted sales demand for Buttercup is 50% less than that of Rose. Budgeted total fixed costs are £52,000.

Complete the table below (to two decimal places) to show the budgeted contribution per unit for the three products and the company's budgeted profit or loss for the year.

	Rose (£)	*Tulip* (£)	*Buttercup* (£)	*Total* (£)
Selling price per unit				
Less: Variable costs per units				
Direct material				
Direct labour				
Contribution per unit				
Sales volume (units)				
Total contribution				
Less: fixed costs				
Budgeted profit/loss				

44 **Sport Shirts Ltd has provided the following cost and sales information for a new range and an existing range of sports shirts:**

	New	*Existing*
Sales and production units	2,000	3,000
Labour hours per month	500	1,500
Unit selling price	£12.00	£20.00
Unit material cost	£3.75	£4.00
Unit direct labour cost	£1.25	£2.50

The company expects its monthly fixed costs to be as follows:

- Production £11,400
- Sales £12,100
- Administration £10,250

Complete the table below to calculate the forecast total monthly contribution and total profit for the company from the sale and production of both shirt ranges

	New £	*Existing* £	*Total* £
Sales Revenue			
Less: variable costs			
Direct materials			
Direct labour			
Total contribution			
Less: fixed costs			
Budgeted profit/loss			

SHORT TERM DECISION MAKING

COST VOLUME PROFIT ANALYSIS

45 Cartcycle Ltd has the following budgeted costs per unit for product MR13:

		£
Variable costs	Direct material	7.50
	Direct labour	8.00
	Overheads	11.50
Total variable costs		27.00
Fixed costs	Overheads	7.20
Total costs		34.20

Product MR13 has a selling price of £41.40 per unit. Budgeted sales volume is 9,000 units.

(a) **Calculate the budgeted fixed overheads for product MR13.**

£

(b) **Calculate the budgeted breakeven volume, in units, for product MR13.**

units

(c) **Complete the table below to show the budgeted margin of safety in units and the margin of safety percentage if Cartcyle Ltd sells 9,000 units of product MR13.**

Units of MR13 sold	9,000
Margin of safety (units)	9000-4500 = 4500
Margin of safety percentage (2dp)	0.50

(d) **If Cartcyle Ltd increases the selling price of MR13 by £1.80 what will be the impact on the breakeven point and the margin of safety assuming no change in the number of units sold?**

A The breakeven point will decrease and the margin of safety will increase

B The breakeven point will stay the same but the margin of safety will decrease

C The breakeven point will decrease and the margin of safety will stay the same

D The breakeven point will increase and the margin of safety will decrease

Cartcycle Ltd wishes to make a profit of £36,000 on the sale of MR13

(e) **Complete the table below to calculate the number of units that Cartcycle Ltd must sell to achieve its target profit, the margin of safety (%) and the margin of safety in sales revenue for the target profit assuming that the sales demand, selling price and all costs remain as per budget.**

	Product MR13
Number of units to be sold to meet target profit	
Revised margin of safety (%)	
Revised margin of safety in sales revenue (£)	

46 Seafood soup sells for 80p per can. It has a marginal cost of production of 30p per can. Fixed costs attributable to this range of soups total £312,500.

(a) **Calculate the sales revenue of seafood soup CCS has to achieve to break even.**

£

(b) **Calculate the sales revenue of seafood soup CCS needs to achieve to make a profit of £200,000.**

£

(c) **If CCS were to sell £875,000 worth of seafood soup, what would be:**

(i) **the margin of safety**

£

(ii) **the margin of safety percentage over the break-even sales?**

%

47 **The following budgeted annual sales and cost information relates to labelled food containers types A and B:**

Product	*A*	*B*
Units made and sold	300,000	500,000
Machine hours required	60,000	40,000
Sales revenue (£)	450,000	600,000
Direct materials (£)	60,000	125,000
Direct labour (£)	36,000	70,000
Variable overheads (£)	45,000	95,000

Total fixed costs attributable to A and B are budgeted to be £264,020.

(a) **Complete the table below (to 2 decimal places) to show the budgeted contribution per unit of A and B sold, and the company's budgeted profit or loss for the year from these two products.**

	A (£)	*B* (£)	*Total* (£)
Selling price per unit			
Less: variable costs per unit			
Direct materials			
Direct labour			
Variable overheads			
Contribution per unit			
Sales volume (units)			
Total contribution			
Less: fixed costs			
Budgeted profit or loss			

The £264,020 of fixed costs attributed to products A and B can be split between the two products: £158,620 to A and £105,400 to B.

The latest sales forecast is that 250,000 units of product A and 400,000 units of product B will be sold during the year.

(b) **Using your calculations and the additional data above, complete the table below to calculate:**

Product	A	B
Fixed costs (£)		
Unit contribution (£)		
Break-even sales (units)		
Forecast sales (units)		
Margin of safety (units)		
Margin of safety (%)		

(c) **Which of the 2 products has the safer margin of safety?**

Product A		Product B	

48 Eastern Bus Company (ECB) has produced three forecasts of miles to be driven during the next three months for a particular contract. The original contract is for journeys totalling 10,000 miles. It now seems likely, however, that the total journeys involved will increase to either 12,000 or 14,000 miles.

(a) **Complete the table below in order to estimate the profit per mile (in pounds, to 3 decimal places) of this contract for the three likely mileages.**

Likely miles	10,000	12,000	14,000
	£	£	£
Sales revenue	100,000		
Variable costs:			
• Fuel	8,000		
• Drivers' wages and associated costs	5,000		
• Overheads	6,000		
Fixed costs:			
• Indirect labour	10,600		
• Overheads	25,850		
Total cost	55,450		
Total profit	44,550		
Profit per mile	4.455		

(b) **Using the information provided above and your own calculations for that task, calculate:**

Forecast number of miles		12,000	14,000
Sales revenue	£		
Fixed costs	£		
Contribution	£		
Contribution per mile	£		
Break-even number of miles	Miles		
Break-even sales revenue	£		
Margin of safety in number of miles	Miles		
Margin of safety in sales revenue	£		
Margin of safety	%		

49 Four lines representing expected costs and revenues have been drawn on a breakeven chart:

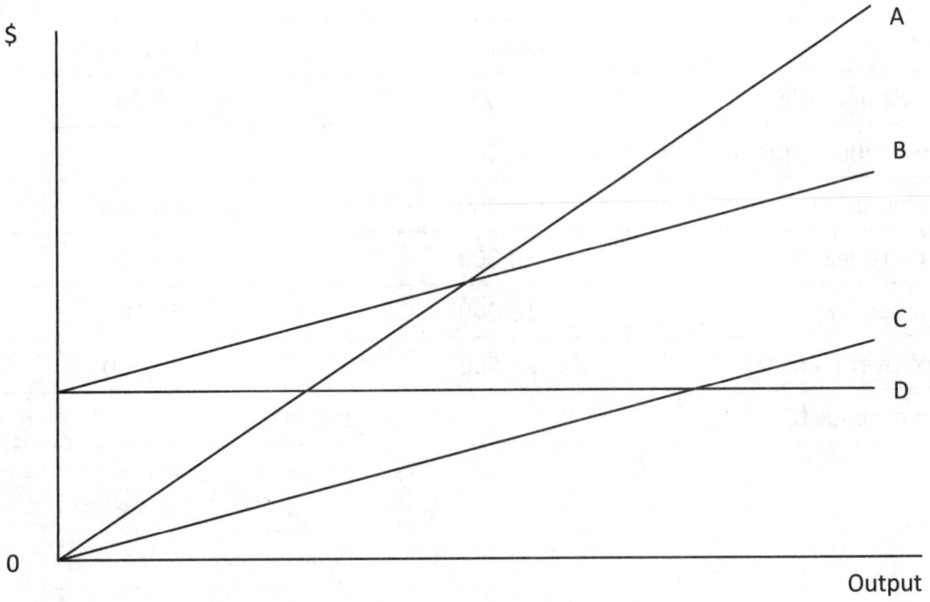

Match the line letter with the correct description?

A
B
C
D

Fixed costs
Total revenue
Total costs
Total variable costs

LIMITING FACTOR ANALYSIS

50 A company manufactures two products (L and M) using the same material and labour. It holds no inventory. Information about the variable costs and maximum demands are as follows:

	Product L	*Product M*
Material (litre)	3.25	4.75
Labour (hour)	5	4
Maximum monthly demand (units)	6,000	8,000

Each month 50,000 litres of material and 60,000 labour hours are available.

Which one of the following statements is correct?

A Material is a limiting factor but labour is not a limiting factor

B Material is not a limiting factor but labour is a limiting factor

C Neither material nor labour is a limiting factor

D Both material and labour are limiting factors

51 Yeknom makes two products, the apple breakfast bar and the banana breakfast bar. The following budgeted annual sales and cost information relates to a and b:

Product	*Apple bars*	*Banana bars*
Bars made and sold	75,000	125,000
Machine hours required	30,000	20,000
Sales revenue(£)	225,000	300,000
Direct materials (£)	30,000	62,500
Direct labour (£)	18,000	35,000
Variable overheads (£)	22,500	47,500
Fixed overheads (£)	150,000	

(a) **Complete the table below (to 2 decimal places) to show the budgeted contribution per bar of Apple and bar of Banana sold, and the company's budgeted profit or loss for the year from these two products.**

	Apple (£)	*Banana* (£)	*Total* (£)
Selling price per bar			
Less: variable costs per unit			
Direct materials			
Direct labour			
Variable overheads			
Contribution per unit			
Sales volume (bars)			
Total contribution			
Less: fixed costs			
Budgeted profit or loss			

Due to a machine breakdown the number of machine hours available for products Apple bars and Banana bars has now been reduced to only 35,000 during the year.

(b) **Given this limitation and your calculations, complete the table below to recommend how many bars of products Apple and Banana Yeknom should now make in order to maximise the profit from these two products for the year.**

Product	*Apple bars*	*Banana bars*	*Total*
Contribution/unit (£)			
Machine hours/unit			
Contribution/machine hour (£)			
Product ranking			
Machine hours available			
Machine hours allocated to: Product .... Product			
Units made			
Total contribution			
Less: fixed costs (£)			
Profit/loss made (£)			

52 **Monty makes two products, the Squeaker and the Hooter. The following budgeted annual sales and cost information relates to the Squeaker and the Hooter:**

Product	*Squeaker*	*Hooter*
Units made and sold	80,000	70,000
Machine hours required	40,000	17,500
Sales revenue(£)	100,000	122,500
Direct materials (£)	40,000	17,500
Direct labour (£)	20,000	35,000
Variable overheads (£)	20,000	45,500
Fixed overheads (£)	15,000	

(a) **Complete the table below (to 2 decimal places) to show the budgeted contribution per bar of Squeakers and Hooters sold, and the company's budgeted profit or loss for the year from these two products.**

	Squeaker (£)	*Hooter* (£)	*Total* (£)
Selling price per bar			
Less: variable costs per unit			
Direct materials			
Direct labour			
Variable overheads			
Contribution per unit			
Sales volume (bars)			
Total contribution			
Less: fixed costs			
Budgeted profit or loss			

Due to a machine breakdown the number of machine hours available for production has now been reduced to only 50,000 during the year.

(b) **Given this limitation and your calculations, complete the table below to recommend how many units of Squeakers and Hooters Monty should now make in order to maximise the profit from these two products for the year.**

Product	*Squeakers*	*Hooters*	*Total*
Contribution/unit (£)			
Machine hours/unit			
Contribution/machine hour (£)			
Product ranking			
Machine hours available			
Machine hours allocated to: Product .... Product			
Units made			
Total contribution			
Less: fixed costs (£)			
Profit/loss made (£)			

53 Three of CPL's products use the same rare plant extract as part of their manufacture. The sole supplier has informed CPL that, due to flooding at its South American facility, they can only supply 6,000 kgs of the plant extract next month.

The following is the budget information about the three affected products for next month:

Product	*AB1*	*CD2*	*EF3*	*Total*
	£	£	£	£
Contribution	26,400	34,600	48,204	109,204
Fixed costs allocated or apportioned	7,430	9,750	13,600	30,780
Profit	18,970	24,850	34,604	78,424
Number of packs to be sold	6,600	6,920	16,068	
Kgs of plant extract required	2,640	1,730	8,034	

Complete the table below to advise how many packs of each product should actually be produced next month to maximise profits during this period.

Product	*AB1*	*CD2*	*EF3*	*Total*
Contribution/pack (£)				
Kgs of plant extract/pack				
Contribution/kg (£)				
Product ranking				
Kgs of plant extract available				
Kgs allocated to each product				
Number of packs to produce				
Total contribution earned (£)				
Less: Fixed costs (£)				
Profit/loss made (£)				

54 **Asparagus soup and broccoli soup have the following budgeted annual sales and cost information:**

Product	*Asparagus soup*	*Broccoli soup*
Cans made and sold	1,200,000	1,800,000
Machine hours required	6,000	9,000
Sales revenue (£)	720,000	900,000
Direct materials (£)	84,000	108,000
Direct labour (£)	72,000	126,000
Variable overheads (£)	24,000	54,000
Fixed overheads attributable to both types of soup (£)	652,000	

(a) **Complete the table below (in pence) to show the budgeted contribution per can for both types of soup, and the company's budgeted profit or loss for the year from these two products (in £).**

	Asparagus soup	*Broccoli soup*	
	p	p	
Selling price per can			
Less: variable costs per can			
Direct materials			
Direct labour			
Variable overheads			
Contribution per can			
	No of cans	No of cans	
Sales volume (cans)			
	£	£	*Total* (£)
Total contribution			
Less: fixed costs			
Budgeted profit or loss			

Due to a machine breakdown the number of machine hours available for production has now been reduced to only 12,000 during the year.

(b) **Given this limitation and your calculations, complete the table below to recommend how many cans of Asparagus soup and Broccoli soup CPL should now make in order to maximise the profit from these two products for the year.**

Product	*Asparagus soup*	*Broccoli soup*	*Total*
Contribution/can (£)			
Machine hours/can			
Contribution/machine hour (£)			
Product ranking			
Machine hours available			
Machine hours allocated to: Product .... Product			
Units made			
Total contribution			
Less: fixed costs (£)			
Profit/loss made (£)			

TYPES OF COSTING SYSTEMS

JOB, BATCH AND SERVICE COSTING

55 A company operates a job costing system. Job 812 requires £60 of direct materials, £40 of direct labour and £20 of direct expenses. Direct labour is paid £8 per hour. Production overheads are absorbed at a rate of £16 per direct labour hour and non-production overheads are absorbed at a rate of 60% of prime cost.

What is the total cost of Job 812?

A £240

B £260

C £272

D £320

56 A business operates a batch costing system. The prime cost of a batch was £6,840 and it had used 156 direct labour hours. The fixed production overheads are absorbed on the basis of direct labour hours. The budgeted overhead absorption rate was based upon a budgeted fixed overhead of £300,000 and total budgeted direct labour hours of 60,000. The batch contained 500 items.

What is the cost per unit in the batch?

£

57 A hotel calculates a number of statistics including average cost per occupied bed per day.

The following information is provided for a 30-day period.

	Rooms with twin beds	*Single rooms*
Number of rooms in hotel	260	70
Number of rooms available to let	240	40
Average number of rooms occupied daily	200	30
Number of guests in period	6,450	
Average length of stay	2 days	
Payroll costs for period	£100,000	
Cost of cleaning supplies in period	£5,000	
Total cost of laundering in period	£22,500	

The average cost per occupied bed per day for the period is:

A £9.90

B £9.88

C £7.20

D £8.17

58 **Which of the following are features of service organisations?**

(i) High levels of inventory

(ii) High proportion of fixed costs

(iii) Difficulty in identifying suitable cost units

A (i) and (ii) only

B (i) and (iii) only

C (ii) and (iii) only

D All of these

PROCESS COSTING – LOSSES

59 The Wood finishing department of Cartcyle Ltd uses process costing for some of its products.

The process account for July for one particular process has been partly completed but the following information is also relevant:

Two employees worked on this process during July. Each employee worked 40 hours per week for 4 weeks and was paid £18 per hour.

Overheads are absorbed on the basis of £28.80 per labour hour.

Cartcyle Ltd expects a normal loss of 5% during this process, which it then sells for scrap at £1.08 per kg.

(a) **Complete the process account below for July. Show total costs to the nearest £ and unit costs to 3 decimal places**

Description	*Kgs*	*Unit cost £*	*Total cost £*		*Description*	*Kgs*	*Unit cost £*	*Total cost £*
Material TR	1,080	2.16			Normal loss		1.08	
Material DG	720	2.70			Output	2,300		
Material IG	720	1.10						
Labour								
Overheads								

(b) **Identify the correct entry for each of the following in a process account.**

	Debit	*Credit*
Abnormal loss		
Abnormal gain		

60 In process costing, if an abnormal loss arises the process account is generally:

A debited with the scrap value of the abnormal loss units

B debited with the full production cost of the abnormal loss units

C credited with the scrap value of the abnormal loss units

D credited with the full production cost of the abnormal loss units

61 The metal finishing department of Aquarius Ltd uses process costing for its product.

The material requirements are:

Material CBB – 700 kilograms @ £1.30 per kilogram

Material BSS – 500 kilograms @ £1.12 per kilogram

Material SMA – 500 kilograms @ £0.72 per kilogram

(a) **Complete the table below (to two decimal places) to show the total cost of the materials input into the process.**

	£
Material CBB	
Material BSS	
Material SMA	

Aquarius Ltd estimate that the process two employees to work on this process. Each employee will work 40 hours per week for 4 weeks and be paid £8 per hour.

Overheads are absorbed on the basis of £12 per labour hour.

(b) **Calculate the total labour cost and total overhead cost**

Total labour cost £	*Total overhead cost £*

(c) **Calculate the total quantity and value of inputs into the process**

Total quantity (kg)	*Total cost £*

Aquarius Ltd expects a normal loss of 2% during this process, which it then sells for scrap at 50p per kg.

(d) **Calculate the total scrap value of the normal loss to 2 decimal places**

Value of scrap £

(e) **Calculate the cost per kilogram of output assuming a normal loss of 2% of input. State your answer to 3 decimal places.**

Cost per kilogram £

(f) **If output is 1,600 calculate if there has been an abnormal loss or gain, the quantity of the loss or gain and the value of the loss**

Abnormal loss or gain	*Quantity of loss or gain* (kg)	*Value of loss or gain* (£)

62 The Glazing department of Grape Ltd uses process costing for glazing finished statues.

The process account for January for one particular process has been partly completed but the following information is also relevant:

Four employees worked on this process during January. Each employee worked 30 hours per week for 4 weeks and was paid £12 per hour.

Overheads are absorbed on the basis of £8 per labour hour.

Grape Ltd expects a normal loss of 10% during this process, which it then sells for scrap at £5 per kg.

Complete the process account below for January. Show total costs to the nearest £ and unit costs to 2 decimal places

Description	*Units*	*Unit cost £*	*Total cost £*		*Description*	*Units*	*Unit cost £*	*Total cost £*
Input – Statues	300	11.25	3,375		Normal loss		5.00	
Materials – Glaze			500		Output	290		
Labour								
Overheads								

63 Last month one of CPL's products had the following process inputs:

- Direct materials — 500 kgs at £17.20 per kg
- Direct labour — 280 labour hours at £10.50 per hour
- Overheads absorbed — 86 machine hours at £32 per machine hour

The following information is also available:

- The company expects a normal loss of 5% of input.
- All waste is sold for £1.68 per kg.
- Actual output for the month was 490 kgs.
- There were no opening or closing inventory and all output was fully completed.

(a) **Calculate the product's cost per kg of normal production.**

£ per kg

(b) **Prepare the process account below for the product for last month:**

Description	*Kgs*	*Unit cost £*	*Total cost £*		*Description*	*Kgs*	*Unit cost £*	*Total cost £*
Materials					Output			
Labour					Normal loss			
Overheads								

PROCESS COSTING – EQUIVALENT UNITS

64 Bahadra makes biscuits. Production requires several successive processes and the production details of the first process are as follows:

Volume completed in period	5,000 kg
Closing work in process	600 kg
Degree of completion of closing WIP:	
Materials	100%
Labour	50%
Overheads	50%
Costs incurred in April:	
Materials	£56,000
Labour	£26,500
Overheads	£10,600

Calculate the cost per equivalent units for materials and conversion

	Materials	*Conversion*
Cost per EU		

65 Parry makes bungee cords. Production requires several successive processes and the production details of the first process are as follows.

Volume completed in period	9,000 units
Closing work in process	3,500 units
Degree of completion of closing WIP:	
Materials	100%
Labour	75%
Overheads	75%
Costs incurred in April:	
Materials	£18,750
Labour	£12,415
Overheads	£16,415

Calculate the cost per equivalent units for materials and conversion

	Materials	*Conversion*
Cost per EU		

66 The following data relates to work in progress stocks of solvent S789 during November:

Opening work in progress	Nil
Finished output to next process	7,000 litres
Closing work in progress	1,200 litres
Degree of completion – direct materials	100%
Degree of completion – direct labour	50%

The total labour cost is £3,800.

The direct labour cost per litre of solvent S789 of the equivalent finished production is:

A £0.46

B £0.50

C £0.60

D £0.63

67 Diamond makes graphite pencils on a production line. The details of the process in Period 2 are as follows:

Opening WIP = 250 units

Costs incurred so far (i.e. value of opening WIP)

Materials £54,000

Conversion £42,000

Degrees of completion

Materials 100%

Conversion 60%

Completed output = 3,200 units

Costs incurred in Period 2:

Materials £123,900

Conversion £91,500

Calculate the cost per equivalent unit using the FIFO method of valuing WIP

	Material	*Conversion*
Cost per EU		

68 Squid makes fountain pens on a production line. The details of the process in Period 2 are as follows:

Opening WIP = 400 units

Costs incurred so far

Materials £115

Conversion £270

Degrees of completion

Materials 100%

Conversion 60%

Completed output = 800 units

Costs incurred in Period 2:

Materials £212

Conversion £448

The cost per equivalent unit for materials and conversion using the FIFO method of valuing WIP:

	Materials	*Conversion*
A	£0.27	£0.47
B	£0.53	£0.70
C	£0.53	£0.80
D	£0.82	£1.28

69 **Silver makes key rings on a production line. The details of the process in period 2 are as follows:**

OWIP = 250 units

Costs incurred so far

Materials	£53,800
Conversion	£42,000

Degrees of completion

Materials	100%
Conversion	60%

Completed output = 3,200 units

Costs incurred in Period 2:

Materials	£135,000
Conversion	£98,800

Calculate the cost per equivalent unit using the AVCO method of valuing WIP

Equivalent units	*Material*	*Conversion*
Cost per EU		

70 **A factory manufactures fizzy drinks. During October work commenced on 11,000 litres.**

OWIP = 2,000 litres

Costs incurred so far

Materials	£400
Conversion	£150

Degrees of completion

Materials	100%
Conversion	50%

Completed output = 9,000 litres

Costs incurred in Period:

Materials	£950
Conversion	£750

The cost per equivalent unit for materials and conversion using AVCO to value OWIP are:

	Material	*Conversion*
A	£6.67	£10
B	£6.67	£11
C	£0.15	£0.09
D	£0.15	£0.10

ABSORPTION AND MARGINAL COSTING

71 Which of the following are true of marginal costing?

(i) The marginal cost of a product includes an allowance for fixed production costs.

(ii) The marginal cost of a product represents the additional cost of producing an extra unit.

(iii) If the inventory increases over a year, the profits under absorption costing will be lower than with marginal costing.

A (i) only

B (ii) only

C (ii) and (iii) only

D (i), (ii) and (iii)

72 Which of these statements are true of marginal costing?

(i) The contribution per unit will be constant if the sales volume increases.

(ii) There is no under–or over–absorption of overheads.

(iii) Marginal costing does not provide useful information for decision making.

A (i) and (ii) only

B (ii) and (iii) only

C (ii) only

D (i), (ii) and (iii)

73 The following information relates to a contract for transporting school children during May 20X7:

	£
Fuel and other variable overheads	9,200
Fixed costs:	
Drivers' wages, pension and national insurance	3,220
Other fixed overheads	23,000
Number of miles travelled	4,600

Calculate the cost per mile under:

(a) Marginal costing

£

(b) Absorption costing

£

74 Globe Ltd has prepared a forecast for the next quarter for Tomato fertilizer.

Globe budgets to produce 1,800kg of the fertiliser and sell 1,000kg. The cost and revenue for this budget is as follows:

	£000
Sales	50,000
Direct materials	7,560
Direct labour	17,640
Fixed Production Overheads	3,600
Advertising (fixed cost)	2,010

Globe has no opening inventory of the fertilizer.

Produce a marginal costing statement of profit or loss and an absorption costing statement of profit or loss

Marginal Costing	£000	£000
Sales		
Opening inventory		
Production costs		
Less: Closing inventory		
Less: Cost of sales		
Contribution		
Less: Fixed costs		
Profit for the period		

Absorption Costing	£000	£000
Sales		
Opening inventory		
Production costs		
Less: Closing inventory		
Lee: Cost of sales		
Gross Profit		
Less: Non-production cost		
Profit for the period		

75 ILCB has the following information relating to one of its products:

- Selling price per unit — £12
- Prime cost per unit — £4
- Variable production cost per unit — £3
- Budgeted fixed production overhead — £30,000 per month
- Budgeted production — 15,000 units per month
- Budgeted sales — 12,000 units per month
- Opening inventory — 2,000 units

(a) **Produce a marginal costing statement of profit or loss**

Marginal Costing	£	£
Sales		
Opening inventory		
Production costs		
Less: Closing inventory		
Less: Cost of sales		
Contribution		
Less: Fixed costs		
Profit for the period		

(b) **What would the profit be under absorption costing principles?**

£

76 CPL is considering what the effect would be of costing its products under marginal costing principles, instead of under absorption costing principles that it currently follows:

The following information relates to one of the company's products:

- Selling price per unit — £40
- Prime cost per unit — £12
- Variable production overhead cost per unit — £4
- Budgeted fixed production overhead — £120,000 per month
- Budgeted production — 12,000 units per month
- Budgeted sales — 10,000 per month
- Opening inventory — 500 units

(a) **Calculate the contribution per unit:**

£

(b) **Calculate the profit per unit:**

£

(c) **Complete the table below to produce a statement of profit or loss for the product for the month under absorption costing principles.**

	£	£
Sales		
Opening inventory		
Variable production costs		
Less: Closing inventory		
Less: Cost of sales		
Contribution		
Less: Fixed costs		
Profit		

(d) **What would the profit be under marginal costing principles?**

£

77 A new company has set up a marginal costing system and has a budgeted profit for the period of £23,000 based on sales of 13,000 units and production of 15,000 units. This level of production represents the firm's expected long-term level of production. The company's budgeted fixed production costs are £3,000 for the period.

If the company were to change to an absorption costing system the budgeted profit would be:

A £22,600

B £23,400

C £25,600

D £26,400

BASIC VARIANCE ANALYSIS

VARIANCE ANALYSIS

78 **Which of the following statements are correct?**

(i) An adverse variance increases profit

(ii) A favourable variance increases profit

(iii) A favourable variance will arise when actual revenue is greater than budgeted revenue

(iv) An adverse variance will arise when actual costs are greater than budgeted costs

Options:

A (i) only

B (ii) only

C (i), (iii) and (iv)

D (ii), (iii) and (iv)

79 Aquarius Ltd. has the following original budget and actual performance for product Britz for the year ending 31 December.

	Budget	*Actual*
Volume sold	200,000	267,000
	£000	£000
Sales revenue	1,600	2,409
Less costs:		
Direct materials	400	801
Direct labour	200	267
Overheads	600	750
Operating profit	400	591

Both direct materials and direct labour are variable costs, but the overheads are fixed

Complete the table below to show a flexed budget and the resulting variances against this budget for the year. Show the actual variance amount, for sales and each cost, in the column headed 'Variance' and indicate whether this is Favourable or Adverse by entering F or A in the final column. If neither F nor A enter 0.

	Flexed budget	*Actual*	*Variance*	*Favourable F or Adverse A*
Volume sold		267,000		
	£000	£000	£000	
Sales revenue		2,409		
Less costs:				
Direct materials		801		
Direct labour		267		
Overheads		750		
Operating profit		591		

80 Grape Ltd. has the following original budget and actual performance for product Bird Box Sets for the year ending 31 December.

	Budget	*Actual*
Volume sold	20,000	28,800
	£000	£000
Sales revenue	3,000	3,877
Less costs:		
Direct materials	175	212
Direct labour	875	912
Overheads	445	448
Operating profit	1,505	2,305

Both direct materials and direct labour are variable costs, but the overheads are fixed

Complete the table below to show a flexed budget and the resulting variances against this budget for the year. Show the actual variance amount, for sales and each cost, in the column headed 'Variance' and indicate whether this is Favourable or Adverse by entering F or A in the final column. If neither F nor A enter 0.

	Flexed budget	*Actual*	*Variance*	*Favourable F or Adverse A*
Volume sold		28,800		
	£000	£000	£000	
Sales revenue		3,877		
Less costs:				
Direct materials		212		
Direct labour		912		
Overheads		448		
Operating profit		2,305		

81 **Globe Ltd. has the following original budget and actual performance for product Bean for the year ending 31 December.**

	Budget	*Actual*
Volume sold (litres)	4,000	5,000
	£000	£000
Sales revenue	1,500	1,950
Less costs:		
Direct materials	36	45
Direct labour	176	182
Overheads	89	90
Operating profit	1,199	1,633

Both direct materials and direct labour are variable costs, but the overheads are fixed

Complete the table below to show a flexed budget and the resulting variances against this budget for the year. Show your answer to the nearest £1000. Show the actual variance amount, for sales and each cost, in the column headed 'Variance' and indicate whether this is Favourable or Adverse by entering F or A in the final column. If neither F nor A enter 0.

	Flexed budget	*Actual*	*Variance*	*Favourable F or Adverse A*
Volume sold		5,000		
	£000	£000	£000	
Sales revenue		1,950		
Less costs:				
Direct materials		45		
Direct labour		182		
Overheads		90		
Operating profit		1,633		

LONG TERM DECISION MAKING

PAYABACK, NPV AND IRR

82 One of the finishing machines in Cartcycle Ltd's Wood finishing department is nearing the end of its useful life and the company is considering purchasing a replacement machine.

Estimates have been made for the initial capital cost, sales income and operating costs of the replacement machine, which is expected to have a useful life of three years:

	Year 0 £000	*Year 1* £000	*Year 2* £000	*Year 3* £000
Capital expenditure	1,620			
Other cash flows:				
Sales income		756	1,008	1,440
Operating costs		216	270	342

The company appraises capital investment projects using a 15% cost of capital.

(a) **Complete the table below and calculate the net present value of the proposed replacement machine (to the nearest £000).**

	Year 0 £000	Year 1 £000	Year 2 £000	Year 3 £000
Capital expenditure				
Sales income				
Operating costs				
Net cash flows				
PV factors	1.0000	0.8696	0.7561	0.6575
Discounted cash flows				
Net present value				

The net present value is *of positive/negative**

*delete as appropriate

(b) **Calculate the payback of the proposed replacement machine to the nearest whole month.**

The payback period is ______Year(s) and _______Months

83 One of the finishing machines in Aquarius Ltd's metal finishing department is nearing the end of its useful life and the company is considering purchasing a replacement machine.

Estimates have been made for the initial capital cost, sales income and operating costs of the replacement machine, which is expected to have a useful life of three years:

	Year 0 £000	Year 1 £000	Year 2 £000	Year 3 £000
Capital expenditure	1,200			
Other cash flows:				
Sales income		530	570	710
Operating costs		140	160	170

The company appraises capital investment projects using a 15% cost of capital.

(a) **Complete the table below and calculate the net present value of the proposed replacement machine (to the nearest £000).**

	Year 0 £000	Year 1 £000	Year 2 £000	Year 3 £000
Capital expenditure				
Sales income				
Operating costs				
Net cash flows				
PV factors	1.0000	0.8696	0.7561	0.6575
Discounted cash flows				
Net present value				

The net present value is *positive/negative**

**delete as appropriate*

(b) **If the net cash inflow in year 4 was £540,000, calculate the payback of the proposed replacement machine to the nearest whole month.**

The payback period is _________Year(s) and ________Months

84 One of the moulding machines in Grape Ltd's Moulding department is nearing the end of its useful life and the company is considering purchasing a replacement machine.

Estimates have been made for the initial capital cost, sales income and operating costs of the replacement machine, which is expected to have a useful life of three years:

	Year 0 £000	*Year 1* £000	*Year 2* £000	*Year 3* £000
Capital expenditure	500			
Other cash flows:				
Sales income		280	330	370
Operating costs		100	120	140

The company appraises capital investment projects using a 10% cost of capital.

(a) **Complete the table below and calculate the net present value of the proposed replacement machine (to the nearest £000).**

	Year 0 £000	*Year 1* £000	*Year 2* £000	*Year 3* £000
Capital expenditure				
Sales income				
Operating costs				
Net cash flows				
PV factors	1.0000	0.909	0.826	0.751
Discounted cash flows				
Net present value				

The net present value is *positive/negative**

**delete as appropriate*

(b) **Estimate the IRR of this project**

A 0%

B 5%

C 10%

D 15%

(c) **Calculate the payback of the proposed replacement machine to the nearest whole month.**

The payback period is ________Year(s) and ________Months

85 Bartrum Ltd is needs to purchase a new mashing machine. There are 2 machines available for purchase. Calculate the net present cost of each machine and recommend which machine should be purchased.

Machine A

	Year 0 £000	Year 1 £000	Year 2 £000	Year 3 £000
Capital expenditure	1,085			
Operating costs		200	200	200

Machine B

	Year 0 £000	Year 1 £000	Year 2 £000	Year 3 £000
Capital expenditure	1,200			
Operating costs		150	160	170

The company appraises capital investment projects using a 15% cost of capital.

Complete the tables below and calculate the net present cost of each of the proposed replacement machines (to the nearest £000).

Machine A

	Year 0 £000	Year 1 £000	Year 2 £000	Year 3 £000
Capital expenditure	1085			
Net cash flows	+1085	-200	-200	200
PV factors	1.0000	0.8696	0.7561	0.6575
Discounted cash flows	-1085	174	151	132
Net present cost	-1542			

Machine B

	Year 0 £000	Year 1 £000	Year 2 £000	Year 3 £000
Capital expenditure	-1200			
Net cash flows	-1200	150	160	170
PV factors	1.0000	0.8696	0.7561	0.6575
Discounted cash flows	-1200	130	121	112.
Net present cost	-1563.			

Bartrum should invest in *Machine A/Machine B**

**delete as appropriate*

86 CPL is considering replacing its fleet of delivery vehicles, and has produced the following estimates of capital expenditure and operating costs for two types of van. Both types of van are expected to have a three-year economic life.

Van type P	Year 0 £000	Year 1 £000	Year 2 £000	Year 3 £000
Capital expenditure	600			
Disposal proceeds				150
Operating costs		275	290	315

Van type R	Year 0 £000	Year 1 £000	Year 2 £000	Year 3 £000
Capital expenditure	750			
Disposal proceeds				170
Operating costs		345	365	390

The company's cost of capital is 16%.

Calculate the net present cost for both types of van. (Round the discounted cash flows to the nearest £000).

The net present cost of van type P

	Year 0 £000	Year 1 £000	Year 2 £000	Year 3 £000
Capital expenditure				
Disposal				
Net cash flows				
PV factors	1.0000	0.8621	0.7432	0.6407
Discounted cash flows				
Net present cost				

The net present cost of van type R

	Year 0 £000	Year 1 £000	Year 2 £000	Year 3 £000
Capital expenditure/disposal				
Net cash flows				
PV factors	1.0000	0.8621	0.7432	0.6407
Discounted cash flows				
Net present cost				

CPL should invest in *Van type P/Van type R**

**delete as appropriate*

87 (a) Globe Ltd's Finance Director has calculated an IRR of 12% for an investment opportunity. The company's required cost of capital is 15%. Should Globe Ltd take this investment opportunity?

Yes/No

(b) Globe Ltd's Finance Director has calculated an IRR of 17% for another investment opportunity. The companies required cost of capital is 15%. Should Globe Ltd take this investment opportunity?

Yes/No

(c) Globe Ltd's Finance Director has calculated an IRR of 15% for an investment opportunity. The companies required cost of capital is 15%. What is the value of the NPV?

£

88 **A company is considering investing in a new mixing machine that will cost £3,000,000 to purchase but will reduce operating costs of the company. The following information is relevant to this decision:**

- The payback period would be 2.4 years. The company's policy is for projects to pay back within 3 years.
- The net present value is £400,000 negative.
- The internal rate of return is 14%. The company's cost of capital is 16%.

Complete the report below, deleting words/phases where appropriate (marked with *)

REPORT

To: The Chief Accountant

From: AAT student

Subject: Investment appraisal

Date: 3 December 20X2

The payback period of 2.4 years is *within/outside** the company's policy of 3 years, and on this criterion the investment *should go/should not go** ahead.

The NPV is *positive/negative** and on this criterion the investment *should go /should not go** ahead.

The IRR, at 14%, is *above/below** the company's 16% cost of capital and on this criterion the investment *should go/should not go** ahead.

Overall the investment *should/should not** proceed because the *Payback/NPV/IRR** is the dominant criterion.

89 **A company has determined that the net present value of an investment project is £17,706 when using a 10% discount rate and £(4,317) when using a discount rate of 15%.**

Calculate the internal rate of return of the project to the nearest 1%.

%

90 **An education authority is considering the implementation of a CCTV (closed circuit television) security system in one of its schools. Details of the proposed project are as follows:**

Life of project 5 years

Initial cost £75,000

Annual savings:

Labour costs £20,000

Other costs £5,000

NPV at 15% £8,800

The discount rates for 20% are:

Year	1	2	3	4	5
PV factors	0.833	0.694	0.579	0.482	0.402

Calculate the internal rate of return for this project to the nearest 1%

A 16%

B 18%

C 20%

D 22%

Section 2

ANSWERS TO PRACTICE QUESTIONS

INVENTORY

1 A

The EOQ formula is $\sqrt{\frac{2 \times \text{cost of ordering} \times \text{annual demand}}{\text{cost of holding one unit for one year}}}$

2 A

The cost of placing an order includes administrative costs, postage and quality control costs

3 **Maximum inventory level:**

Re-order level = max usage × max lead time = 800 × 3 = 2,400

Re-order quantity = 500

Maximum = 2,400 + 500 – (500 × 1) = **2,400 units**

Minimum inventory level:

Re-order level = max usage × max lead time = 800 × 3 = 2,400

Average usage = (500 + 800)/2 = 650

Average lead time = (1 + 3)/2 = 2 weeks

Minimum = 2,400 – (650 × 2) = **1,100 units**

4 (a) The EOQ = $\sqrt{\frac{2 \times 3.60 \times 112{,}500}{1.80}} = 671$

(b) Inventory record card

	Receipts			**Issues**			**Balance**	
Date	*Quantity kgs*	*Cost per kg (£)*	*Total cost (£)*	*Quantity kgs*	*Cost per kg (p)*	*Total cost (£)*	*Quantity kgs*	*Total cost (£)*
Balance as at 22 July							198	238
24 July	671	2.336	1,567				869	1,805
26 July				540	1.920	1,037	329	768
28 July	671	2.344	1,573				1,000	2,341
30 July				710	2.341	1,662	290	679

Workings

Issue on 26th July is made up of 198 @ 1.202 and 342 @ 2.336

Issue on 30th July is made up of 329 @ 2.336 and 391 @ 2.344

(d) 540 × £2.336 = **£1,261**

5 SURESTICK GLUE

(a) The EOQ = $\sqrt{\dfrac{2 \times 2.50 \times 2{,}500 \times 12}{1.00}} = 388$

(b) Inventory record card

	Receipts			**Issues**			**Balance**	
Date	*Quantity litres*	*Cost per litre*	*Total cost (£)*	*Quantity litres*	*Cost per litre*	*Total cost (£)*	*Quantity Litres*	*Total cost (£)*
Balance as at 23 June							65	130
24 June	388	2.234	867				453	997
26 June				180	2.201	397	273	600
27 June	388	2.341	909				661	1,509
30 June				250	2.283	571	411	938

(d) 180 × £2.234 = **£402**

6 GRAPE LTD

(a) **C** – AVCO

(b) Inventory record card

	Receipts			**Issues**			**Balance**	
Date	*Drums*	*Cost per Drum (£)*	*Total cost (£)*	*Drums*	*Cost per drum (p)*	*Total cost (£)*	*Drums*	*Total cost (£)*
Balance as at 22 January							1,650	1,980
25 January	1,200	1.250	1,500				2,850	3,480
26 January				1,300	1.221	1,587	1,550	1,893
28 January	1,200	1.302	1,562				2,750	3,455
31 January				1,500	1.256	1,884	1,250	1,571

7 GLOBE LTD

(a) **A** – FIFO

(b) Inventory record card

	Receipts			Issues			Balance	
Date	*Tonnes*	*Cost per tonne (£)*	*Total cost (£)*	*Tonnes*	*Cost per tonne (£)*	*Total cost (£)*	*Tonnes*	*Total cost (£)*
Balance as at 27 March							1,200	14,400
28 March	800	12.50	10,000				2,000	24,400
29 March				820	12.00	9,840	1,180	14,560
30 March	800	12.25	9,800				1,980	24,360
31 March				900	12.29	11,060	1,080	13,300

Working

Issue on 31st March is made up of 380 @ 12 and 520 @12.50

8 **A** – FIFO

9 **A**

When prices are rising, FIFO will give a higher valuation for closing inventory, because the closing inventory will consist of the most recently-purchased items. Higher closing inventory means lower cost of sales and higher profit.

JOURNAL ENTRIES

INVENTORY

10 **C**

Materials inventory account

	£000s		£000s
Opening inventory	15	Issued to production	165
Payables for purchases	176	Returned to suppliers	8
Returned to stores	9	Written off	4
		Closing balance (balancing item)	23
	–––		–––
	200		200

11

	Choice
Transaction 1	(C) Dr. Inventory, Cr. Bank
Transaction 2	(F) Dr. Production, Cr. Inventory
Transaction 3	(D) Dr. Inventory, Cr. Trade payables' Control
Transaction 4	(E) Dr. Inventory, Cr. Production

12

	Choice
Transaction 1	(D) Dr. Inventory, Cr. Trade payables' Control
Transaction 2	(F) Dr. Statement of profit or loss, Cr. Inventory
Transaction 3	(C) Dr. Inventory, Cr. Bank
Transaction 4	(B) Dr. Trade payables' Control, Cr. Inventory

13 B

Indirect materials are overhead costs so debit production overhead. An issue of materials is a credit from the material control account

LABOUR

14 (a) **The wages control account entries**

Wages control account

	£		£
Bank (net wages/salaries)	10,000	Maintenance (direct labour)	7,000
HMRC (income tax and NIC)	2,000	Maintenance overheads	4,000
Pension contribution	1,000	Maintenance administration	2,000
	13,000		**13,000**

(b) **The total payroll cost charged to the various cost accounts of the business**

Date	Code	Debit	Credit
30 November	8200		7,000
30 November	6200	7,000	
30 November	8200		4,000
30 November	6400	4,000	
30 November	8200		2,000
30 November	6600	2,000	

15

	Choice
Transaction 1	(A) Dr. Wages control, Cr. Bank
Transaction 2	(B) Dr. Work-in-progress, Cr. Wages control
Transaction 3	(C) Dr. Production overhead account, Cr. Wages Control
Transaction 4	(D) Dr. Production overhead control, Cr. Bank

OVERHEADS

16 D

Over-absorbed overheads increase profit, and so are recorded as a credit entry in either an over-absorbed overhead account or directly as a credit in the income statement. The matching debit entry could be either in the WIP account or the production overhead control account, depending on the costing system used.

17 C

Indirect labour is a costing concept. The double entry is:

Wages control		**Overhead control**	
	Indirect labour × (overheads)	Indirect labour × (wages)	

LABOUR COSTS

LABOUR

18 CARTCYLE LTD

Employee's weekly timesheet for week ending 7 December

Employee:	A. Man		**Profit Centre:**	Wood finishing		
Employee number:	C812		**Basic pay per hour:**	£8.00		
	Hours spent on production	*Hours worked on indirect work*	*Notes*	*Basic pay £*	*Overtime premium £*	*Total pay £*
Monday	6	2	10am–12am cleaning of machinery	64	8	72
Tuesday	2	4	9am–1pm customer care course	48	0	48
Wednesday	8			64	8	72
Thursday	6			48	0	48
Friday	6	1	3–4pm health and safety training	56	4	60
Saturday	6			48	24	72
Sunday	3			24	24	48
Total	**37**	**7**		352	68	420

Alternative

Sunday	3			0	48	48
Total	**37**	**7**		328	92	420

19 (a)

	Units
Actual production	5,400,000
Standard production (5,000 hours at 800 units)	(4,000,000)
Excess production	1,400,000
Bonus %	$\frac{25\% \times 1{,}400{,}000}{4{,}000.000} = 8.75\%$
Group bonus rate per hour	0.0875 × £10 = £0.875
Total group bonus	5,000 hours at £0.875 = £4,375

(b) Basic pay 44 hours at £9.60 = £422.40

Bonus pay 44 hours at £0.875 = £38.50

Total pay £460.90

20 GRAPES

Employee's weekly timesheet for week ending 31 January

Employee:	Olivia Michael		**Profit Centre:**	Moulding Department		
Employee number:	P450		**Basic pay per hour:**	£10.00		
	Hours spent in work	*Hours worked on indirect work*	*Notes*	*Basic pay* £	*Overtime premium* £	*Total pay* £
Monday	8	3	10am–1pm cleaning moulds	80	5	85.00
Tuesday	7	4	9am–1pm fire training	70	0	70.00
Wednesday	8			80	5	85.00
Thursday	7	1		70	0	70.00
Friday	7	1	3–4pm annual appraisal	70	0	70.00
Saturday	3			30	7.50	37.50
Total	**40**	**9**		400	17.50	417.50

Labour cost account

	£		£
Bank	417.50	Production	310
		Production Overheads	107.50

Production is direct labour only therefore basic hours less time spent on non-production activities:

(40 – 9) × £10 = £310

Production overheads are the indirect costs therefore the cost is:

£17.50 + (9 × £10) = £107.50

21 (a) **The correct total cost of direct labour for the bottles is:**

Cost at normal rate:	1,215 hours at £8 =	£9,720
Cost at time and a half:	180 hours at £4 =	£720
Cost at double time:	135 hours at £8 =	£1,080
Total direct labour cost		£11,520
Alternative calculation:		
Cost at normal rate:	900 hours at £8 =	£7,200
Cost at time and a half:	180 hours at £12 =	£2,160
Cost at double time:	135 hours at £16 =	£2,160
Total direct labour cost		£11,520

(b) **The cost of direct labour per bottle is:**

Total direct labour cost:	£11,520
Divided by number of bottles	57,600
Cost of direct labour per bottle	£0.20

22 **C**

Product	*Quantity*	*Standard time per item (hours)*	*Total Standard time (hours)*
Buckles	50	0.2	10
Press studs	200	0.06	12
Belts	100	0.1	10
Buttons	10	0.7	7
			39

39 hours × £8 per hour = £312

23 (a)

Total basic pay (£)	10,800 × 9 = £97,200
Total overtime premium (£)	2,450 × 5.50 = £13,475
Hours saved (hours)	400
Bonus (£)	400 × 9 × 0.35 = £1,260
Total direct labour cost (£)	£111,935

(b)

Equivalent units	Completed CWIP 200 × 0.75 EU	300 150 —— 450
Bonus (£)		0

ACCOUNTING FOR OVERHEADS

OVERHEAD ALLOCATION AND APPORTIONMENT

24 D

Cost apportionment is concerned with sharing costs according to benefit received.

25 CARTCYLE LTD

	Basis of apportionment	*Wood cutting* £	*Wood finishing* £	*Maintenance* £	*Stores* £	*General Admin* £	*Totals* £
Depreciation of plant and equipment	CA of plant and equipment	1,013,229	434,241	–	–	–	1,447,470
Power for production machinery	Production machinery power usage (KwH)	772,200	514,800	–	–	–	1,287,000
Rent and rates	Floor space	–	–	94,050	56,430	37,620	188,100
Light and heat	Floor space	–	–	20,790	12,474	8,316	41,580
Indirect labour	Allocated	–	–	182,070	64,890	432,180	679,140
Totals		1,785,429	949,041	296,910	133,794	478,116	3,643,290

	Basis of apportionment	*Wood cutting* £	*Wood finishing* £	*Maintenance* £	*Stores* £	*General Admin* £	*Totals* £
Reapportion Maintenance		207,837	89,073	(296,910)			
Reapportion Stores		86,966	46,828		(133,794)		
Reapportion General Admin		239,058	239,058			(478,116)	
Total overheads to production centres		2,319,290	1,324,000				3,643,290

26 CARTCYLE LTD

	Basis of apportionment	*Assembly* £	*Finishing* £	*Maintenance* £	*Stores* £	*General Admin* £	*Totals* £
Depreciation of plant and equipment	CA of plant and equipment	420,000	280,000	–	–	–	700,000
Power for production machinery	Production machinery power usage (KwH)	403,000	217,000	–	–	–	620,000
Rent and rates	Floor space	–	–	48,000	32,000	20,000	100,000
Light and heat	Floor space	–	–	9,600	6,400	4,000	20,000
Indirect labour	Allocated	–	–	102,000	40,000	240,000	382,000
Totals		823,000	497,000	159,600	78,400	264,000	1,822,000
Reapportion Maintenance		88,000	88,000	52,800	35,200	(264,000)	
Reapportion Stores		56,800	34,080	22,720	(113,600)		
Reapportion General Admin		176,340	58,780	(235,120)			
Total overheads to production centres		1,144,140	677,860				1,822,000

27

	Basis of apportionment	*Scheduled services*	*Charter flights*	*Aircraft maintenance and repairs*	*Fuel and parts store*	*General Admin* £	*Totals* £
		£000	£000	£000	£000	£000	£000
Depreciation of aircraft	CA of aircraft	21,840	14,560	–	–	–	36,400
Aviation fuel and other variables	Planned number of miles flown	23,210	18,990	–	–	–	42,200
Pilots and aircrew salaries	Allocated	5,250	4,709	–	–	–	9,959
Rent and rates and other premises costs	Floor space	–	–	6,300	3,780	2,520	12,600
Indirect labour	Allocated	–	–	9,600	3,200	7,800	20,600
Totals		50,300	38,259	15,900	6,980	10,320	121,759
Reapportion Maintenance and repairs		9,540	6,360	(15,900)			
Reapportion fuel and parts store		3,839	3,141		(6,980)		
Reapportion General Admin		5,160	5,160			(10,320)	
Total overheads to profit centres		68,839	52,920				121,759

28

	Basis of apportionment	*Plastics Moulding*	*Labelling*	*Stores*	*Equipment Maintenance*	*Totals*
Heat and lighting fixed cost	Allocated	6,000	6,000	6,000	6,000	24,000
Heat and lighting variable cost	Square meters occupied	19,200	10,800	4,800	1,200	36,000
Power for machinery	Percentages	19,600	8,400	–	–	28,000
Supervision	Direct labour cost	50,000	70,000	–	–	120,000
Stores wages	Allocated	–	–	72,000	–	72,000
Equipment maintenance salaries	Allocated	–	–	–	188,200	188,200
Depreciation of non-current assets	CA of non-current assets	48,000	24,000	9,000	3,000	84,000
Other overhead costs	Percentages	76,800	25,600	12,800	12,800	128,000
Totals		219,600	144,800	104,600	211,200	680,200
Reapportion Maintenance		70,400	70,400	70,400	(211,200)	
Reapportion Stores		130,200	44,800	(175,000)		
Total overheads to profit centres		420,200	260,000			680,200

OVERHEAD ABSORPTION

29 C

An absorption rate is used to determine the full cost of a product or service. Answer A describes overhead allocation and apportionment. Absorption does not control overheads, so answer D is not correct.

30 (a) OAR = 586,792/9,464 = £62

The correct answer is A

(b) Absorbed = 62 × 9,745 = £604,190

The correct answer is C

(c) Over absorption = 604,190 – 568,631 = £35,559 over absorbed

The correct answer is A

31 (a) Assembly = 155,000/2,000 = £77.50 and Finishing = 105,000/1,750 = £60

The correct answer is B

(b) Assembly = 155,000/12,500 = £12.40 and Finishing = 105,000/8,750 = £12

The correct answer is D

(c) Absorbed overhead = 1,750 × 90% hours × £60 = £94,500

Therefore **£24,500 under** absorbed

32 (a) Moulding = 36,000/18,000 = £2 and Painting = 39,000/13,000 = £3

The correct answer is D

(b) Moulding = £2 × 17,500 = £35,000 and Painting = £3 × 13,500 = £40,500

The correct answer is A

(c) Moulding = 35,000 – 37,500 = £2,500 under absorbed and Painting = 40,500 – 40,000 = 500 over absorbed.

The correct answer is B

33 (a) Mixing = 64,800/10,000 = £6.48 and Bagging = 70,200/2,340 = £30.00

The correct answer is A

(b) Mixing = £6.48 × 9,000 = £58,320 and Bagging = £30.00 × 2,120 = £63,600

The correct answer is C

(c) Mixing = 58,320 – 67,500 = £9,180 under absorbed and Bagging = 63,600 – 75,600 = £12,000 under absorbed.

The correct answer is B

34 **A**

Under–or over-absorption is determined by comparing the actual overhead expenditure with the overhead absorbed.

35 **D**

Fixed production overheads are over-absorbed when actual expenditure is less than budget and/or actual production volume is higher than budget.

ACTIVITY EFFECTS

COST BEHAVIOURS

36 C

	£
Total cost of 18,500 hours	251,750
Total cost of 17,000 hours	246,500
Variable cost of 1,500 hours	5,250

Variable cost per machine hour = £5,250/1,500 machine hours = £3.50.

	£
Total cost of 17,000 hours	246,500
Less variable cost of 17,000 hours (× £3.50)	59,500
Balance = fixed costs	187,000

37 A

	Cost per unit (£) *(125 units)*	*Cost per unit* (£) *(180 units)*
T1	8.00	7.00
T2	14.00	14.00
T3	19.80	15.70
T4	25.80	25.80

Cost types T2 and T4 are variable and T1 and T3 are semi-variable.

38 Graph 1 C; Graph 2 D

39 *Direct* costs are ones that can be economically and exclusively identified with a cost unit. Examples include *Fabric* used in production of clothing and *Electrical components* used in the manufacture of computers.

Indirect costs, or *Overheads*, are costs that cannot be economically and exclusively identified with a cost unit. Examples include *Light, heat and power costs.*

40

Batches produced and sold	**2,160**	**2,700**	**3,600**
	£	£	£
Sales revenue	64,800	81,000	108,000
Variable costs:			
• **Direct materials**	9,720	12,150	16,200
• **Direct labour**	22,680	28,350	37,800
• **Overheads**	12,960	16,200	21,600
Semi-variable costs:	6,804		
• **Variable element**		5,400	7,200
• **Fixed element**		2,484	2,484
Total cost	52,164	64,584	85,284
Total profit	12,636	16,416	22,716
Profit per batch (to 2 decimal places)	5.85	6.08	6.31

41

Likely miles	**5,000**	**6,000**	**7,000**
	£000	£000	£000
Sale revenue	2,500	2,950	3,400
Variable/semi-variable costs:			
• **Aviation fuel**	400	480	560
• **Landing and servicing fees**	850	900	950
• **Other variable overheads**	135	162	189
Fixed costs:			
• **Wages and salaries**	420	420	420
• **Other fixed overheads**	625	625	625
Total cost	2430	2,587	2,744
Total profit	70	363	656
Profit per mile flown (2 d.p.) £	14.00	60.50	93.71

42 (a) **£24,000 ÷ 800** = £30

(b) VC = £3,600 + £8,400 + £1,800 = £13,800

VC per unit = £13,800 ÷ 800 = £17.25

SV VC per unit = (£4,920 – £2,520) ÷ (1,600 – 800) = £3.00

Total VC per unit = **£20.25**

(c) FC = £2,520 – (800 × 3) = £120

FC per unit = £120 ÷ 1,200 = **£0.10**

(d) Total cost = (£20.25 × 1,500) + 120 = £30,495

Total cost per unit = £30,495 ÷ 1,500 = **£20.33**

(e) Contribution per unit = £30 – £20.25 = £9.75

Total contribution = £9.75 × 1,500 = £14,625

Total profit = £14,625 – £120 = £14,505

Profit per unit = £14,505 ÷ 1,500 = **£9.67**

SEGMENTAL REPORTS

43

	Rose (£)	*Tulip* (£)	*Buttercup* (£)	*Total* (£)
Selling price per unit	50.00	120.00	80.00	
Less: Variable costs per units				
Direct material	10.00	24.00	16.00	
Direct labour	13.00	44.00	21.00	
Contribution per unit	27.00	52.00	43.00	
Sales volume (units)	1,000	200	500	
Total contribution	27,000	10,400	21,500	58,900
Less: fixed costs				52,000
Budgeted profit				6,900

44

	New £	*Existing* £	*Total* £
Sales Revenue	24,000	60,000	
Less: variable costs			
Direct materials	7,500	12,000	
Direct labour	2,500	7,500	
Total contribution	14,000	40,500	54,500
Less: fixed costs			33,750
Budgeted profit			20,750

SHORT TERM DECISION MAKING

COST VOLUME PROFIT ANALYSIS

45 (a) **£7.20 × 9,000 = £64,800**

(b) $\frac{64{,}800}{41.40 - 27} = 4{,}500$ units

(c)

Units of MR 13 sold	**9,000**
Margin of safety (units)	9,000 – 4,500 = 4,500 units
Margin of safety percentage	$\frac{9{,}000 - 4{,}500}{9{,}000} \times 100 = 50\%$

(d) The correct answer is **A** – an increase in selling price means that contribution per unit increases therefore fewer units have to be made to cover the fixed costs. If BEP is lower than the margin of safety is higher.

(e)

	Product MR13
Number of units to be sold to meet target profit	$\frac{£36{,}000 + £64{,}800}{£14.40} = 7{,}000$ units
Revised margin of safety (%)	$\frac{9{,}000 - 7{,}000}{9{,}000} \times 100 = 28.57\%$
Revised margin of safety in sales revenue (£)	2,000 × £41.40 = £82,800

46 (a) $\frac{£312,500}{£0.50/£0.80} = £500,000$

(b) $\frac{£312,500 + £200,000}{£0.50/£0.80} = £820,000$

(c) (i) £875,000 – £500,000 = £375,000

(ii) £375,000/£500,000 × 100 = 75%

47 (a)

	A (£)	*B* (£)	*Total* (£)
Selling price per unit	1.50	1.20	
Less: variable costs per unit			
Direct materials	0.20	0.25	
Direct labour	0.12	0.14	
Variable overheads	0.15	0.19	
Contribution per unit	1.03	0.62	
Sales volume (units)	300,000	500,000	
Total contribution	309,000	310,000	619,000
Less: fixed costs			264,020
Budgeted profit or loss			354,980

(b)

Product	*A*	*B*
Fixed costs (£)	158,620	105,400
Unit contribution (£)	1.03	0.62
Break-even sales (units)	154,000	170,000
Forecast sales (units)	250,000	400,000
Margin of safety (units)	96,000	230,000
Margin of safety (%)	38.40	57.50

(c)

Product A		Product B	✓

48 (a)

Likely miles	10,000	12,000	14,000
	£	£	£
Sales revenue	100,000	120,000	140,000
Variable costs:			
• Fuel	8,000	9,600	11,200
• Drivers' wages and associated costs	5,000	6,000	7,000
• Overheads	6,000	7,200	8,400
Fixed costs:			
• Indirect labour	10,600	10,600	10,600
• Overheads	25,850	25,850	25,850
Total cost	55,450	59,250	63,050
Total profit	44,550	60,750	76,950
Profit per mile	4.455	5.063	5.496

(b)

Forecast number of miles			14,000
Sales revenue	£	120,000	140,000
Fixed costs	£	36,450	
Contribution	£	97,200	
Contribution per mile	£	8.10	
Break-even number of miles	Miles	4,500	
Break-even sales revenue	£	45,000	
Margin of safety in number of miles	Miles	7,500	9,500
Margin of safety in sales revenue	£	75,000	95,000
Margin of safety	%	62.50	67.90

49 Line A is total revenue

Line B is total costs

Line C is total variable costs

Line D is fixed costs

LIMITING FACTOR ANALYSIS

50 D

Material required to meet maximum demand:

(6,000 × 3.25) + (8,000 × 4.75) = 57,500 litres

Material available: 50,000 litres

∴ Material is a limiting factor

Labour required to meet maximum demand:

(6,000 × 5) + (8,000 × 4) = 62,000 hours

Labour available: 60,000 hours

∴ Labour is a limiting factor

51 (a)

	Apple (£)	*Banana* (£)	*Total* (£)
Selling price per bar	3.00	2.40	
Less: variable costs per unit			
Direct materials	0.40	0.50	
Direct labour	0.24	0.28	
Variable overheads	0.30	0.38	
Contribution per unit	2.06	1.24	
Sales volume (bars)	75,000	125,000	
Total contribution	154,500	155,000	309,500
Less: fixed costs			150,000
Budgeted profit or loss			159,500

(b)

Product	*Apple bars*	*Banana bars*	*Total*
Contribution/unit (£)	2.06	1.24	
Machine hours/unit	0.40	0.16	
Contribution/machine hour (£)	5.15	7.75	
Product ranking	2	1	
Machine hours available			35,000
Machine hours allocated to: Product: Banana Product : Apple	15,000	20,000	
Units made	37,500	125,000	
Total contribution	77,250	155,000	232,250
Less: fixed costs (£)			150,000
Profit/loss made (£)			82,250

52 (a)

	Squeaker (£)	*Hooter* (£)	*Total* (£)
Selling price per unit	1.25	1.75	
Less: variable costs per unit			
Direct materials	0.50	0.25	
Direct labour	0.25	0.50	
Variable overheads	0.25	0.65	
Contribution per unit	0.25	0.35	
Sales volume (units)	80,000	70,000	
Total contribution	20,000	24,500	44,500
Less: fixed costs			15,000
Budgeted profit			29,500

(b)

Product	*Squeaker*	*Hooter*	*Total*
Contribution/unit (£)	0.25	0.35	
Machine hours/unit	0.50	0.25	
Contribution/machine hour (£)	0.50	1.40	
Product ranking	2	1	
Machine hours available			50,000
Machine hours allocated to: Product: Hooter Product : Squeaker	32,500	17,500	
Units made	65,000	70,000	
Total contribution	16,250	24,500	40,750
Less: fixed costs (£)			15,000
Profit made (£)			25,750

53

Product	*AB1*	*CD2*	*EF3*	*Total*
Contribution/pack (£)	4.00	5.00	3.00	
Kgs of plant extract/pack	0.40	0.25	0.50	
Contribution/kg (£)	10	20	6	
Product ranking	2	1	3	
Kgs of plant extract available				6,000
Kgs allocated to each product	2,640	1,730	1,630	
Number of packs to produce	6,600	6,920	3,260	
Total contribution earned (£)	26,400	34,600	9,780	70,780
Less: Fixed costs (£)				30,780
Profit/loss made (£)				40,000

54 (a)

	Asparagus soup	*Broccoli soup*	
	p	p	
Selling price per can	60	50	
Less: variable costs per can			
Direct materials	7	6	
Direct labour	6	7	
Variable overheads	2	3	
Contribution per can	45	34	
	No of cans	No of cans	
Sales volume (cans)	1,200,000	1,800,000	
	£	£	*Total* (£)
Total contribution	540,000	612,000	1,152,000
Less: fixed costs			652,000
Budgeted profit or loss			500,000

(b)

Product	*Asparagus soup*	*Broccoli soup*	*Total*
Contribution/can (£)	0.45	0.34	
Machine hours/can	0.005	0.005	
Contribution/machine hour (£)	90	68	
Product ranking	1	2	
Machine hours available			12,000
Machine hours allocated to: Product: Asparagus Soup Product : Broccoli Soup	6,000	6,000	
Units made	1,200,000	1,200,000	
Total contribution	540,000	408,000	948,000
Less: fixed costs (£)			652,000
Profit/loss made (£)			296,000

TYPES OF COSTING SYSTEMS

JOB, BATCH AND SERVICE COSTING

55 C

	Job 812
	£
Direct materials	60
Direct labour	40
Direct expenses	20
Prime cost	120
Production overheads (£40 ÷ 8) × £16	80
Non-production overheads (0.6 × £120)	72
Total cost – Job 812	272

56 C

		£
Prime cost		6,840.00
Fixed overhead	£300,000 ÷ 60,000 × 156	780.00
		7,620.00

Cost per unit = 7,620 ÷ 500 = **£15.24**

57 B

Average cost per occupied bed per day

$$= \frac{\text{Total cost}}{\text{Number of beds occupied}}$$

$$= \frac{£100{,}000 + £5{,}000 + £22{,}500}{6{,}450 \times 2} = £9.88$$

or £127,500/(200 × 2 + 30) × 30 = £9.88

58 C

A service is intangible and inventory cannot be held. Services generally have a high level of fixed costs and there are often difficulties in identifying a suitable cost unit.

PROCESS COSTING – LOSSES

59

Description	*Kg's*	*Unit cost £*	*Total cost £*		*Description*	*Kg's*	*Unit cost £*	*Total cost £*
Material TR10	1,080	2.16	2,333		Normal loss	126	1.08	136
Material DG41	720	2.70	1,944		Output	2,300	8.316	19,127
Material IG11	720	1.10	792		Abnormal loss	94	8.316	782
Labour			5,760					
Overheads			9,216					
	2,520		20,045			2,520		20,045

(b)

	Debit	*Credit*
Abnormal loss		✓
Abnormal gain	✓	

60 **D**

Abnormal loss units are valued as one equivalent unit of cost, the same as units of good production. This cost is credited to the process account and debited to the abnormal loss account. The scrap value of abnormal loss is then credited to the abnormal loss account (with the matching debit to bank).

61 (a) **Complete the table below (to two decimal places) to show the total cost of the materials input into the process.**

	£
Material CBB	910
Material BSS	560
Material SMA	360

(b) **Calculate the total labour cost and total overhead cost**

Total labour cost £	*Total overhead cost £*
2,560	3,840

(c) **Calculate the total quantity and value of inputs into the process**

Total quantity (kg)	*Total cost* £
1,700	8,230

(d) **Calculate the total scrap value of the normal loss to 2 decimal places**

Value of scrap £
(1,700 × 2%) × 0.50 = £17.00

(e) **Calculate the cost per kilogram of output assuming a normal loss of 2% of input. State your answer to 3 decimal places.**

Cost per kilogram £
(£8,230 – £17) ÷ (1,700 – 34) = £4.93

(f) **If output is 1,600 calculate if there has been an abnormal loss or gain, the quantity of the loss or gain and the value of the loss (to the nearest £)**

Abnormal loss or gain	*Quantity of loss or gain (kg)*	*Value of loss or gain*
Abnormal loss	1,700 – 1,600 – 34 = 66	66 × £4.93 = £325

62

Description	*Units*	*Unit cost* £	*Total cost* £		*Description*	*Units*	*Unit cost* £	*Total cost* £
Input – Statues	300	11.25	3,375		Normal loss	30	5.00	150
Materials – Glaze			500		Output	290	49.35	14,312
Labour			5,760					
Overheads			3,840					
Abnormal gain	20	49.35	987					
	320		14,462			320		14,462

63 (a)

$$\frac{(500 \times 17.20) + (280 \times 10.50) + (86 \times 32) - (500 \times 5\% \times 1.68)}{500 - (500 \times 5\%)} = £30$$

(b)

Description	*Litres*	*Cost per litre* £	*Total cost* £		*Description*	*Litres*	*Cost per litre* £	*Total cost* £
Materials	500	17.20	8,600		Output	490	30.00	14,700
Labour			2,940		Normal loss	25	1.68	42
Overheads			2,752					
Abnormal gain	15	30.00	450					
	515		14,742			515		14,742

PROCESS COSTING – EQUIVALENT UNITS

64 **Statement of EU**

	Materials	*Conversion*
Completed	5,000	5,000
CWIP	600	300
TOTAL EU	5,600	5,300
Costs		
Period Costs	56,000	26,500
		10,600
TOTAL COSTS	56,000	37,100
Cost per EU	10.00	7.00

65 **Statement of EU**

	Materials	*Conversion*
Completed	9,000	9,000
CWIP	3,500	2,625
TOTAL EU	12,500	11,625
Costs		
Period Costs	18,750	12,415
		16,415
TOTAL COSTS	18,750	28,830
Cost per EU	1.50	2.48

66 B

Statement of EU

	Labour
Completed (7,000 × 100%)	7,000
CWIP (1,200 × 50%)	600
TOTAL EU	7,600
Costs	
Period Costs	3,800
TOTAL COSTS	3,800
Cost per EU	0.50

67 Statement of EU

Note: Using FIFO so the EU calculation focuses on costs incurred and work done this period.

	Materials	*Conversion*
OWIP to complete	0	100
Completed output	2,950	2,950
TOTAL EU	2,950	3,050
Costs		
Period Costs	123,900	91,500
TOTAL COSTS	123,900	91,500
Cost per EU	42	30

68 C

Note: Using FIFO so the EU calculation focuses on costs incurred and work done this period.

Equivalent units		*Material*	*Conversion*
	OWIP to complete	0	160
	Completed Output	400	400
	Total EU	400	560
Costs			
	Period	212	448
	Total cost	212	448
Cost per EU		0.53	0.80

69 **Note:** Using AVCO so the EU calculation will include all costs (including those b/f in OWIP) and all output, not just the work done this period.

Equivalent units		*Material*	*Conversion*
	Completed Output	3,200	3,200
	Total EU	3,200	3,200
Costs			
	OWIP	53,800	42,000
	Period	135,000	98,800
	Total cost	188,800	140,800
Cost per EU		59	44

70 **D**

Note: Using AVCO so the EU calculation will include all costs (including those b/f in OWIP) and all output, not just the work done this period.

Equivalent units		*Material*	*Conversion*
	Completed Output	9,000	9,000
	Total EU	9,000	9,000
	OWIP	400	150
	Period	950	750
	Total cost	1,350	900
Cost per EU		0.15	0.10

ABSORPTION AND MARGINAL COSTING

71 **B**

The marginal cost of a product is the additional cost of producing an extra unit and is therefore the sum of the variable costs. If the inventory increases over a year, absorption costing profit will be higher than marginal costing profit because an element of fixed cost will be carried forward in closing inventory to be charged against profit in a future period.

72 **A**

Total contribution will increase as sales volume increases, but the contribution per unit will be constant as long as the sales price and variable cost per unit are unchanged. Overhead is not absorbed into the product unit so there is no under/over absorption of overhead. Marginal costing *does* provide useful information for decision making because it highlights contribution, which is a relevant cash flow for decision-making purposes.

73 **The cost per mile under:**

(a) **Marginal costing**

Fuel and other variable overheads	*£ per mile*
Total variable cost per mile £9,200/4,600 miles	**2.00**

(b) **Absorption costing**

Fuel and other variable overheads	*£ per mile*
Total variable cost per mile £9,200/4,600 miles	2.00
Drivers' wages, pension and national insurance £3,220/4,600 miles	0.70
Fixed overheads £23,000/4,600 miles	5.00
Total absorption cost per mile	**7.70**

74 **Marginal costing**

	£000	£000
Sales		50,000
Opening inventory	0	
Production costs (7,560 + 17,640)	25,200	
Closing inventory (25,200/1,800 × 800)	–11,200	
Cost of sales		–14,000
Contribution		36,000
Fixed costs (3,600+2010)		–5,610
Profit for the period		30,390

Absorption costing

	£000	£000
Sales		50,000
Opening inventory	0	
Production costs (7,560 + 17,640 + 3,600)	28,800	
Closing inventory (28,800/1,800 × 800)	–12,800	
Cost of sales		–16,000
Gross Profit		34,000
Non-production cost		–2,010
Profit for the period		31,990

75 (a) **Marginal Costing**

	£	£
Sales (12 × 12,000)		144,000
Opening inventory (7 × 2,000)	14,000	
Production costs (7 × 15,000)	105,000	
Closing inventory (7 × 5,000)	–35,000	
Cost of sales		–84,000
Contribution		60,000
Fixed costs		–30,000
Profit for the period		30,000

(b) **Reconcile the two profits:**

Absorption costing profit	**36,000**
Change in inventory × OAR (2,000 – 5,000) × (30,000/15,000)	–6,000
Marginal costing profit	30,000

76 (a)

	£
Selling price/unit	40
Prime cost/unit	(12)
Variable production cost/unit	(4)
Contribution/unit	24

(b)

	£
Selling price/unit	40
Marginal cost/unit	(16)
Fixed production cost/unit (£120,000/12,000 units)	(10)
Profit/unit	14

(c)

Absorption Costing

	£	£
Sales (40 × 10,000)		400,000
Opening inventory (26 × 500)	13,000	
Production costs (26 × 12,000)	312,000	
Closing inventory (26 × 2,500)	–65,000	
Cost of sales		–260,000
Profit for the period		140,000

(d) **Reconcile the two profits:**

Absorption costing profit	140,000
Change in inventory × OAR (500 – 2,500) × 10	–20,000
Marginal costing profit	**120,000**

77 B

In an absorption costing system, the fixed cost per unit would be £3,000/15,000 units = £0.20 per unit.

By switching to absorption costing, in a period when inventory levels increase by 2,000 units, absorption costing profit would be higher by 2,000 units × fixed cost per unit, i.e. by 2,000 × £0.20 = £400.

Absorption costing profit = £23,000 + £400 = £23,400.

BASIC VARIANCE ANALYSIS

VARIANCE ANALYSIS

78 D

79

	Flexed budget	*Actual*	*Variance*	*Favourable F or Adverse A*
Volume sold	267,000	267,000		
	£000	£000	£000	
Sales revenue	2,136	2,409	273	F
Less costs:				
Direct materials	534	801	267	A
Direct labour	267	267	0	0
Overheads	600	750	150	A
Operating profit	735	591	144	A

80

	Flexed budget	*Actual*	*Variance*	*Favourable F or Adverse A*
Volume sold	28,800	28800		
	£000	£000	£000	
Sales revenue	4,320	3,877	443	A
Less costs:				
Direct materials	252	212	40	F
Direct labour	1,260	912	348	F
Overheads	445	448	3	A
Operating profit	2,363	2,305	58	A

81

	Flexed budget	*Actual*	*Variance*	*Favourable F or Adverse A*
Volume sold	5,000	5,000		
	£000	£000	£000	
Sales revenue	1,875	1,950	75	F
Less costs:				
Direct materials	45	45	0	0
Direct labour	220	182	38	F
Overheads	89	90	1	A
Operating profit	1,521	1,633	112	F

LONG TERM DECISION MAKING

PAYBACK, NPV AND IRR

82 (a)

	Year 0 £000	*Year 1* £000	*Year 2* £000	*Year 3* £000
Capital expenditure	–1,620			
Sales income		756	1,008	1,440
Operating costs		–216	–270	–342
Net cash flows	–1,620	540	738	1,098
PV factors	1.0000	0.8696	0.7561	0.6575
Discounted cash flows	–1,620	470	558	722
Net present value	130			

The net present value is **positive**

(b)

Year	*Cash flow* £000	*Cumulative cash flow* £000
0	(1,620)	(1,620)
1	540	(1,080)
2	738	(342)
3	1,098	756

The payback period is **2** years and **4** months.

Months = 342/1,098 × 12 = 3.7 months

83 (a)

	Year 0 £000	*Year 1* £000	*Year 2* £000	*Year 3* £000
Capital expenditure	–1,200			
Sales income		530	570	710
Operating costs		–140	–160	–170
Net cash flows	–1,200	390	410	540
PV factors	1.0000	0.8696	0.7561	0.6575
Discounted cash flows	–1,200	339	310	355
Net present value	–196			

The net present value is **negative**

(b)

Year	*Cash flow* £000	*Cumulative cash flow* £000
0	(1,200)	(1,200)
1	390	(810)
2	410	(400)
3	540	140

The payback period is **2** years and **9** months.

Months = 400/540 × 12 = 8.9 months

84 (a)

	Year 0 £000	*Year 1* £000	*Year 2* £000	*Year 3* £000
Capital expenditure	–500			
Sales income		280	330	370
Operating costs		–100	–120	–140
Net cash flows	–500	180	210	230
PV factors	1.0000	0.909	0.826	0.751
Discounted cash flows	–500	164	173	173
Net present value	10			

The net present value is **positive**

(b) **D**

(c)

Year	*Cash flow* £000	*Cumulative cash flow* £000
0	(500)	(500)
1	180	(320)
2	210	(110)
3	230	120

The payback period is **2** years and **6** months.

Months = 110/230 × 12 = 5.7 months

85 Machine A

	Year 0 £000	*Year 1* £000	*Year 2* £000	*Year 3* £000
Capital expenditure	–1,085			
Net cash flows	–1,085	–200	–200	–200
PV factors	1.0000	0.8696	0.7561	0.6575
Discounted cash flows	–1,085	–174	–151	–132
Net present cost	–1,542			

Machine B

	Year 0 £000	*Year 1* £000	*Year 2* £000	*Year 3* £000
Capital expenditure	–1,200			
Net cash flows	–1,200	–150	–160	–170
PV factors	1.0000	0.8696	0.7561	0.6575
Discounted cash flows	–1,200	–130	–121	–112
Net present cost	–1,563			

Bartrum should invest in **Machine A**

86 Van type P

	Year 0 £000	Year 1 £000	Year 2 £000	Year 3 £000
Capital expenditure	–600			
Disposal				150
Net cash flows	–600	–275	–290	–165
PV factors	1.0000	0.8621	0.7432	0.6407
Discounted cash flows	–600	–237	–216	–106
Net present cost	–1,159			

Van type R

	Year 0 £000	Year 1 £000	Year 2 £000	Year 3 £000
Capital expenditure/disposal	–750			170
Net cash flows	–750	–345	–365	–220
PV factors	1.0000	0.8621	0.7432	0.6407
Discounted cash flows	–750	–297	–271	–141
Net present cost	–1,459			

CPL should invest in **Van type P**

87 (a) **No**

(b) **Yes**

(c) £ Nil

88

REPORT

To: The Chief Accountant

From: AAT student

Subject: Investment appraisal

Date: 3 December 20X2

The payback period of 2.4 years is *within* the company's policy of 3 years, and on this criterion the investment *should go* ahead.

The NPV is *negative** and on this criterion the investment *should not go* ahead.

The IRR, at 14%, is *below* the company's 16% cost of capital and on this criterion the investment *should not go* ahead.

Overall the investment *should not* proceed because the *NPV* is the dominant criterion.

89 14%

$$10 + \frac{£17,706}{(£17,706 - £4,317)} \times (15 - 10) = 14\%$$

90 C

Year	*Cash*	20%	*PV*
	£		£
0	(75,000)		(75,000)
1	25,000	0.833	20,825
2	25,000	0.694	17,350
3	25,000	0.579	14,475
4	25,000	0.482	12,050
5	25,000	0.402	10,050
			(250)

IRR $= 15 + \frac{8,800}{8,800 - (250)} \times 5$

IRR $= 15 + \frac{8,800}{9,050} \times 5$

IRR = 19.86% therefore **20%** to the nearest 1%

Section 3

MOCK QUESTIONS

TASK 1

Sarloue Ltd has the following information available for superfine oil S07:

Date purchased	*Quantity*	*Cost per litre*	*Total cost* (£)
5 July	625	2.20	1,375
16 July	550	2.40	1,320
22 July	650	2.50	1,625

Calculate the cost of an issue of 600 litres on 20 July and the inventory balance at the end of the month (round to the nearest £).

	Cost (£)
AVCO issue	
AVCO balance	
FIFO issue	
FIFO balance	
LIFO issue	
LIFO balance	

TASK 2

Put the correct entries into the Journal below to record the following FOUR accounting transactions:

1 Receipt of oil into inventory paying by cheque.

2 Issue of oil from inventory to production.

3 Receipt of oil into inventory paying on credit.

4 Return of oil from inventory to supplier who had sold oil on credit.

The choices are:

A Dr. Bank, Cr. Inventory

B Dr. Trade Payables' Control, Cr. Inventory

C Dr. Inventory, Cr. Bank

D Dr. Inventory, Cr. Trade Payables' Control

E Dr. Inventory, Cr. Production

F Dr. Production, Cr. Inventory

	Choice
Transaction 1	
Transaction 2	
Transaction 3	
Transaction 4	

TASK 3

Below is a weekly timesheet for one of Sarloue Ltd's employees, who is paid as follows:

- For a basic seven and a half hour shift every day from Monday to Friday – basic pay.
- For any overtime in excess of the basic seven and a half hours, on any day from Monday to Friday – the extra hours are paid at time-and-a-half.
- For any hours worked on Saturday or Sunday – paid at double time.

Complete the columns headed Basic pay, Overtime premium and Total pay:

(***Notes:*** Zero figures should be entered in cells where appropriate).

Employee's weekly timesheet for week ending 21 July

Employee:	A. Lander		**Profit Centre:**	Warehouse store man		
Employee number:	S007		**Basic pay per hour:**	£8.00		
	Total hours spent in work	*Hours spent on indirect work*	*Notes*	*Basic pay £*	*Overtime premium £*	*Total pay £*
Monday	8	½	Late delivery			
Tuesday	7 ½					
Wednesday	8	½	Early delivery			
Thursday	8	½	Cleaning warehouse			
Friday	7 ½					
Saturday	4		Stock taking			
Sunday	2		Stock taking			
Total	**45**	**1 ½**				

TASK 4

Sarloue Ltd's budgeted overheads for the next financial year are:

	£000	£000
Depreciation of plant and equipment		22,250
Power for production machinery		17,500
Rent and rates		23,750
Light and heat		6,250
Indirect labour costs:		
Maintenance	10,000	
Stores	12,500	
Canteen	36,000	
Total indirect labour cost		58,500

The following information is also available:

Department	*Carrying amount of plant and equipment*	*Production machinery power usage (KwH)*	*Floor space (square metres)*	*Number of employees*
Production centres:				
Plastic moulding	180,000	22,500	2,000	20
Plastic extrusion	360,000	30,000	2,000	20
Support cost centres:				
Maintenance			1,000	2
Stores			3,000	2
Canteen			2,000	2
Total	540,000	52,500	10,000	46

Overheads are allocated or apportioned on the most appropriate basis. The total overheads of the support cost centres are then reapportioned on the follow bases:

- 60% of the Maintenance cost centre's time is spent maintaining production machinery in the Plastic moulding production centre and 30% of time is spent in the Plastic extrusion production centre. The remainder is spent maintaining the canteen equipment
- The Stores cost centre supports the two production centres equally
- The Canteen cost centre is reapportioned based on staff numbers

Complete the overhead analysis table below:

	Basis of apportionment	Plastic moulding	Plastic extrusion	Maintenance	Stores	Canteen	Totals
		£000	£000	£000	£000	£000	£000
Depreciation of plant and equipment							
Power for production machinery							
Rent and rates							
Light and heat							
Indirect labour							
Totals							
Reapportion Maintenance							
Reapportion Stores							
Reapportion Canteen							
Total overheads to production centres							

TASK 5

Sarloue Ltd's budgeted overheads and activity levels are:

	Plastic moulding	*Plastic extrusion*
Budgeted overheads (£)	22,500	24,750
Budgeted direct labour hours	5,000	5,200
Budgeted machine hours	15,000	20,000

(a) What would the budgeted overhead absorption rate for each department, if this were set based on being heavily automated, to the nearest penny?

A Plastic moulding £1.50/hour, Plastic extrusion £1.24/hour

B Plastic moulding £1.50/hour, Plastic extrusion £0.62/hour

C Plastic moulding £3/hour, Plastic extrusion £0.62/hour

D Plastic moulding £3/hour, Plastic extrusion £1.24/hour

(b) What would the budgeted overhead absorption rate for each department, if this were set based on being labour intensive, to the nearest penny?

A Plastic moulding £4.50/hour, Plastic extrusion £2.38/hour

B Plastic moulding £4.50/hour, Plastic extrusion £4.76/hour

C Plastic moulding £9/hour, Plastic extrusion £4.76/hour

D Plastic moulding £9/hour, Plastic extrusion £2.38/hour

Additional data

At the end of the quarter actual overheads incurred were found to be:

	Plastic moulding	*Plastic extrusion*
Actual overheads (£)	19,800	28,000

Overheads were recovered on a labour hour basis. The labour hours were 5% more than budgeted in Plastic moulding and 3% more in Plastic extrusion.

(c) Calculate the overhead that was absorbed in each department and state the under or over absorption that occurred in each department (answers to the nearest £)

	Absorbed amount £	*Under/over*	*Value £*
Plastic moulding			
Plastic extrusion			

TASK 6

Sarloue Ltd has prepared a forecast for the next quarter for three of its engineered components, GG57, HH23 and KK12.

The company expects to produce and sell 1,000 GG57 and 1,500 HH23. The budgeted sales demand for KK12 is 25% greater than that of HH23. Budgeted total fixed costs are £12,750

Other budgeted information for the three products is as follows:

Product	*GG57*	*HH23*	*KK12*
Sales revenue (£)	25,000	20,625	20,625
Direct materials (£)	7,500	7,875	5,625
Direct labour (£)	8,750	6,000	3,750

Complete the table below (to TWO decimal places) to show the budgeted contribution per unit of product sold.

	GG57 (£)	*HH23* (£)	*KK12* (£)	*Total* (£)
Selling price per unit				
Less: variable costs per unit:				
• Direct materials				
• Direct labour				
Contribution per unit				
Sales volume (units)				
Total contribution				
Less: fixed cost				
Budgeted profit/loss				

TASK 7

Sarloue has a contract with a customer to produce 5,000 litres of GG99. Revenues and costs for 5,000 litres are shown below.

Possible production level	*5,000 litres*
	£
Sales revenue	145,000
Variable and semi-variable costs:	
Material	30,000
Labour	40,000
Overheads	25,000
Fixed costs:	
Indirect labour	20,000
Overheads	15,000
Target profit for contract	11,500

The labour cost is a semi-variable cost. The fixed cost is £20,000 and the variable cost is £4.00 per unit.

Use the table below to calculate the required number of units for this contract to achieve its target profit. Enter the contribution per mile to two decimal places.

Calculation of required number of litres	£
Fixed costs	
Target profit	
Fixed cost and target profit	
Sales revenue	
Variable costs	
Contribution	
Contribution per unit	
Required number of litres to achieve target profit	

TASK 8

Sarloue uses both batch and unit costing, as appropriate, in its plastic extrusion department. It is currently costing a new product LL45. LL45 will be produced in batches of 4,500.

It has been estimated that the following costs will be incurred in producing on batch of 4,500 units of LL45.

Product LL45	£
Direct materials £ per unit	6.00
Direct labour £ per unit	5.50
Variable overheads £ per batch	14,625
Total fixed manufacturing overheads	36,000
Total fixed administration, selling and distribution costs	19,170

(a) Calculate the prime cost of one unit of LL45

(b) Calculate the marginal cost of one batch of LL45

(c) Calculate the marginal cost of one unit of LL45

(d) Calculate the full absorption cost of one batch of LL45

(e) Calculate the full absorption cost of one unit of LL45

TASK 9

Sarloue Ltd has the following original budget and actual performance for product GG101 for the year ending 31 December.

	Budget	*Actual*
Volume sold	20,000	18,500
Sales revenue	40,000	38,850
Less costs:		
Direct materials	16,000	17,575
Direct labour	10,000	10,175
Overheads	2,000	1,950
Operating profit	12,000	9,150

Both direct materials and direct labour are variable costs, but the overheads are fixed.

Complete the table below to show a flexed budget and the resulting variances against this budget for the year. Show the actual variance amount, for sales and each cost, in the column headed 'Variance' and indicate whether this is Favourable or Adverse by entering F or A in the final column. If neither F nor A enter 0.

	Flexed budget	*Actual*	*Variance*	*Favourable F or Adverse A*
Volume sold		18,500		
Sales revenue		38,850		
Less costs:				
Direct materials		17,575		
Direct labour		10,175		
Overheads		1,950		
Operating profit		9,150		

TASK 10

One of the extrusion machines in the Plastic extrusion department is nearing the end of its useful life and Sarloue Ltd is considering purchasing a replacement machine.

Estimates have been made for the initial capital cost, sales income and operating costs of the replacement machine, which is expected to have a useful life of three years:

	Year 0 £000	*Year 1* £000	*Year 2* £000	*Year 3* £000
Capital expenditure	450			
Other cash flows:				
Sales income		600	650	750
Operating costs		420	480	510

The company appraises capital investment projects using a 15% cost of capital.

(a) Complete the table below and calculate the net present value of the proposed replacement machine (to the nearest £000).

	Year 0 £000	*Year 1* £000	*Year 2* £000	*Year 3* £000
Capital expenditure				
Sales income				
Operating costs				
Net cash flows				
PV factors	1.0000	0.8696	0.7561	0.6575
Discounted cash flows				
Net present value				

The net present value is *positive/negative**

**delete as appropriate*

(b) The IRR for this project will be *greater than/less than** 15%

(c) Calculate the payback of the proposed replacement machine to the nearest whole month.

The payback period is ________Year(s) and ________Months

Section 4

ANSWERS TO MOCK QUESTIONS

TASK 1

	Cost (£)
AVCO issue	1,376
AVCO balance	2,944
FIFO issue	1,320
FIFO balance	3,000
LIFO issue	1,430
LIFO balance	2,890

TASK 2

	Choice
Transaction 1	(C) Dr. Inventory, Cr. Bank
Transaction 2	(F) Dr. Production, Cr. Inventory
Transaction 3	(D) Dr. Inventory, Cr. Trade Payables control
Transaction 4	(B) Dr. Trade Payables control, Cr. Inventory

TASK 3

Employee's weekly timesheet for week ending 21 July

Employee:	A. Lander		**Profit Centre:**	Warehouse store man		
Employee number:	S007		**Basic pay per hour:**	£8.00		
	Total hours spent in work	*Hours spent on indirect work*	*Notes*	*Basic pay* £	*Overtime premium* £	*Total pay* £
Monday	8	½	Late delivery	64	4	68
Tuesday	7½			60	0	60
Wednesday	8	½	Early delivery	64	4	68
Thursday	8	½	Cleaning warehouse	64	4	68
Friday	7 ½			60	0	60
Saturday	4		Stock taking	32	32	64
Sunday*	2		Stock taking	16	16	32
Total	**37**	**1 ½**		360	60	420

* Alternative answer for Sunday

Sunday*	2		Stock taking	0	32	32
Total	**37**	**1 ½**		344	76	420

TASK 4

	Basis of apportionment	*Plastic moulding £000*	*Plastic extrusion £000*	*Maintenance £000*	*Stores £000*	*Canteen £000*	*Totals £000*
Depreciation of plant and equipment	CA of plant and equipment	7,417	14,833	0	0	0	22,250
Power for production machinery	Production machinery power usage (KwH)	7,500	10,000	0	0	0	17,500
Rent and rates	Floor space	4,750	4,750	2,375	7,125	4,750	23,750
Light and heat	Floor space	1,250	1,250	625	1,875	1,250	6,250
Indirect labour	Allocated	0	0	10,000	12,500	36,000	58,500
Totals		20,917	30,833	13,000	21,500	42,000	128,250
Reapportion Maintenance		7,800	3,900	(13,000)		1,300	
Reapportion Stores		10,750	10,750		(21,500)		
Reapportion Canteen		21,650	21,650			(43,300)	
Total overheads to production centres		61,117	67,133				128,250

TASK 5

(a) Plastic moulding = 22,500/15,000 = £1.50 and Plastic extrusion = 24,750/20,000 = £1.24.

The correct answer is A

(b) Plastic moulding = 22,500/5,000 = £4.50 and Plastic extrusion = 24,750/5,200 = £4.76.

The correct answer is B

(c)

	Absorbed amount £	*Under/ over*	*Value £*
Plastic moulding	£4.50 × (5,000 × 1.05) = £23,625	Over	£23,625 – £19,800 = £3,825
Plastic extrusion	£4.76 × (5,200 × 1.03) = £25,495	Under	£28,000 – £25,495 = £2,505

TASK 6

	GG57 (£)	*HH23* (£)	*KK12* (£)	*Total* (£)
Selling price per unit	25.00	13.75	11.00	
Less: variable costs per unit:				
• Direct materials	7.50	5.25	3.00	
• Direct labour	8.75	4.00	2.00	
Contribution per unit	8.75	4.50	6.00	
Sales volume (units)	1,000	1,500	1,875	
Total contribution	8,750	6,750	11,250	26,750
Less: fixed cost				12,750
Budgeted profit/loss				14,000

TASK 7

Calculation of required number of litres	£
Fixed costs	55,000
Target profit	11,500
Fixed cost and target profit	66,500
Sales revenue	145,000
Variable costs	75,000
Contribution	70,000
Contribution per unit	14
Required number of litres to achieve target profit	4,750

TASK 8

(a) **Calculate the prime cost of one unit of LL45**

£6.00 + £5.50 = £11.50

(b) **Calculate the marginal cost of one batch of LL45**

(£11.50 × 4,500) + £14,625 = £66,375

(c) **Calculate the marginal cost of one unit of LL45**

£66,375 ÷ 4,500 = £14.75

(d) **Calculate the full absorption cost of one batch of LL45**

£66,375 + £36,000 = £102,375

(e) **Calculate the full absorption cost of one unit of LL45**

£102,375 ÷ 4,500 = £22.75

TASK 9

	Flexed budget	*Actual*	*Variance*	*Favourable F or Adverse A*
Volume sold	18,500	18,500		
Sales revenue	37,000	38,850	1,850	F
Less costs:				
Direct materials	14,800	17,575	2,775	A
Direct labour	9,250	10,175	925	A
Overheads	2,000	1,950	50	F
Operating profit	10,950	9,150	1,800	A

TASK 10

(a)

	Year 0 £000	*Year 1* £000	*Year 2* £000	*Year 3* £000
Capital expenditure	(450)			
Sales income		600	650	750
Operating costs		(420)	(480)	(510)
Net cash flows	(450)	180	170	240
PV factors	1.0000	0.8696	0.7561	0.6575
Discounted cash flows	(450)	157	129	158
Net present value	(6)			

The net present value is **negative**

(b) The IRR for this project will be **less than** 15%

(c)

Year	*Cash flow* £000	*Cumulative cash flow* £000
0	(450)	(450)
1	180	(270)
2	170	(100)
3	240	140

The payback period is **2** years and **5** months. Months = 100/240 × 12 = 5 months